MW00791851

BOOKS BY ALICE KUIPERS

Dropped (2023)
Polly Diamond and the Topsy-Turvy Day (2023)
Pia's Plans (2020)
World's Worst Parrot (2020)
Always Smile: Carley Allison's Secrets for Laughing, Loving and Living (2019)
Polly Diamond and the Super Stunning Spectacular School Fair (2019)
Polly Diamond and the Magic Book (2018)
Me and Me (2017)
Violet and Victor Write the Most Fabulous Fairytale (2016)
Violet and Victor Write the Best-Ever Bookworm Book (2014)
The Death of Us (2014)
40 Things I Want to Tell You (2012)
The Worst Thing She Ever Did (2010)
Life on the Refrigerator Door (2007)

SPARK

ALICE KUIPERS

ON WRITING FOR KIDS & YOUNG ADULTS

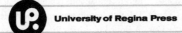

University of Regina Press

Printed and bound in Canada. The text of this book is printed on 100% post-consumer recycled paper with earth-friendly vegetable-based inks.

Cover art: "Sketchy Notebook Doodles" (modified) by blue67 / Adobe Stock
Cover design: Duncan Campbell, University of Regina Press
Interior layout design: John van der Woude, JVDW Designs
Copyeditor: Kelly Laycock
Proofreader: Shannon Parr

Library and Archives Canada Cataloguing in Publication

Title: Spark : Alice Kuipers on writing for kids & young adults.
Names: Kuipers, Alice, 1979- author
Series: Writers on writing (Regina, Sask.)
Description: Series statement: Writers on writing
Identifiers: Canadiana (print) 20240383788 | Canadiana (ebook) 2024038380X | ISBN 9781779400239 (hardcover) | ISBN 9781779400222 (softcover) | ISBN 9781779400246 (PDF) | ISBN 9781779400253 (EPUB)
Subjects: LCSH: Children's literature—Authorship. | LCSH: Young adult literature—Authorship. | LCSH: Children's literature—Technique. | LCSH: Young adult literature—Technique.
Classification: LCC PN147.5 .K85 2024 | DDC 808.06/8—dc23

10 9 8 7 6 5 4 3 2 1

University of Regina Press, University of Regina
Regina, Saskatchewan, Canada, S4S 0A2
TEL: (306) 585-4758 FAX: (306) 585-4699
WEB: www.uofrpress.ca

We acknowledge the support of the Canada Council for the Arts for our publishing program. We acknowledge the financial support of the Government of Canada. / Nous reconnaissons l'appui financier du gouvernement du Canada. This publication was made possible with support from Creative Saskatchewan's Book Publishing Production Grant Program.

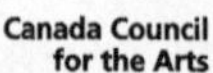

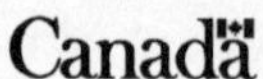

To Louise Dean and Bill Kenower

Both of you in your inimitable, brilliant teaching have shown me how to be fearless and true. I've learned so much from your mentorship, your generosity, and your insights.

Thank you.

CONTENTS

PART 3. REWRITING

INTRODUCTION

YOU AS A STORYTELLER, YOU AS A WRITER

You want to write, and this book is for you. You've picked it up because a tiny voice inside you wants you to write your words down (or you're my friend or family member—either way, thank you!).

That voice, the one that tells you that you want to write, matters.

Writing matters.

As Will Storr explains, "your brain is a storyteller." I take this to mean that we interpret our world through the stories we tell. Some of those stories are simple: I drink coffee every morning, say, making me a coffee drinker. Other stories are more complicated, turning into books of narrative, giving us all clues about how to live.

Perhaps you've got an idea for a book for children, and you don't know much about how books for kids work, yet. Or you loved a young adult novel you read recently, and you're inspired to write one, too. You might have been writing for years or just starting out, you could have a record of publication or have no idea how to begin to send work out into the world. Maybe you've tried writing picture books but you're about to discover that you want to write a middle grade novel.

At this stage, anything is possible, and I want to share everything I know to help you undertake your next steps in the magical world of writing for young readers. Think of the words here as tools to help you flourish, making it as easy and as thrilling as possible for you to get more creativity into your life. Inside you is a spark, and with care, love, and work, you can make that spark flame into a beautiful story.

I share what I've learned and the experiences I've had along the way, because I believe sharing my personal story can help you find yours. Something pulls you to write for young readers: perhaps you have young people in your life, or you love books for children, or both. As you fan the flame of that passion, together we'll explore the rich world of books for kids and young adults. As you read and as you write, you'll discover so many opportunities, and hopefully, each discovery will spark new ideas and possibilities for you as a writer.

HOW THIS BOOK WORKS

This book starts with something I'll call Prewriting. I'll look at where ideas come from, how to read like a writer, and the types of books out there for young readers.

In the Writing section of the book, we build a writing routine before looking at the structure of story itself. You'll learn about character and the elements of scenes. This section finishes with how to write your draft.

Once you've drafted your book, Rewriting begins. Here we explore editing, submissions, and publication (along with its flip side, rejection), and we look at how to live a writing life.

You can read the chapters in order or dip and pick. When I begin reading a book about writing, I'm very keen to get going and actually write. In my experience, there's nothing more thrilling than getting those words on the page in the way you want to, the way you've always dreamed. I've offered some exercises for you that can inspire you and spark ideas.

The exercises are designed for you to work on in your own time and at your own pace. If you follow them in order, you'll have more of the tools you need to write the book you want.

Take your time with each exercise to uncover yourself as a writer. The exercises are there for you when and if you want to do them. Use them if they're helpful. Don't if they're not. As you can see, in each section of exercises there are four steps, designed for wherever you're at in your writing journey. The first step is always a practical task; some involve some writing or thinking, but often these tasks are to help you become more like the writer you most want to be, whether you've been writing for years or you're just starting. The second and third steps are both writing exercises. One is a 10-minute exercise, and often asks you to use a prompt to free-write with. The other is a 30-minute exercise for when you have more writing time. The last step is for those of you who want to take the elements of the chapter further, to dig deeper, and to explore more. All of the steps are for whatever stage of your writing life you're in.

My hope for you is that this book helps you discover for which audience (age group) you want to write, and what your book will be. I'm hoping you'll write a draft and then get it ready for readers. Most of all, I hope you make time for writing and affirm its importance in your life: while you'll hopefully love writing for young readers, you're also writing for *yourself*. This book, like the others in the Writers on Writing series by University of Regina Press, is a balance between talking you through how to write, while sharing with you my own writing life and what I've learned along the way.

Of course, this book can only cover so much. There are many amazing things to learn and continue to learn about writing for children, young adults, and for yourself. This book gives you an overview, and a spark, and is there for you to follow through to get yourself where you want to be. But there's a lot of other material for you, and you will find extensive book lists and resources at the back of this book to continue your learning.

The world is always shifting, so keeping up with the book industry—publishing in all its forms—is a challenge. Generative AI text creation puts together words, bringing with it questions about creativity and the tools you want to use. It's changing every day. And my understanding of writing is always changing, too. But no matter what changes come our way, people need stories, and there will always be those who want to write these stories down. Like you. Local writer Leona Theis said to me recently: "Only you can write your book your way."

Whatever continues to change in the industry, those words remain vital and true.

THE BOOKS I'VE WRITTEN

As I write, I'm sitting in a co-working space on Broadway in Saskatoon, far from the life I thought I'd live. I've published thirteen books with my name on the cover in lots of countries, and several books as a ghost writer. I've had stories turned into plays and produced on the radio, and I've published in the occasional magazine. Through Fiction Express, a publisher that shares chapters week by week with kids who choose where the story goes, I've also published five short novels. I've written at least twenty other books that have either been rejected or never seen; I think at least seven of those are two or three edits from being much stronger, but I don't currently want to do that work—I'll explain that later, promise!

I've written reams online, shared writing classes with thousands of students, both in person and through the internet, and I have four other books on the go. One is this one, now published and in your hands. Another is a book for young readers, published by Orca Book Publishers, and one is a book I'm ghost writing.

The fourth book I'm working on right now is a novel for adults. I've been writing it for two years now, and it may or may not be published. Ever. Despite that, this adult novel has taught me and changed me (like every book I've written), and I'm grateful for it. Whether it becomes something that anyone else can ever read or stays in my computer for me alone, it reminds me how much I still have to learn as a writer and how much is possible.

I mention all these projects not to put you in a panic: you don't need to be working on multiple books at the same time. You don't need to do anything the way I do it. I just want you to know my experience, so you trust what I'm sharing with you is rooted in a writing reality.

I've gathered the material for this book over many years. Although very much changed for this manuscript, some content is from a University of Toronto online course I used to teach, that was later a free eBook. Some of these chapters started as blog posts, or as classes I've taught with *Children's Book Insider*. Some exercises are ones I've created for classes or are based on similar exercises on my website—some years ago, I shared a weekly writing prompt on Wattpad. Much of what is in this book has come from listening to other writers, either working one-on-one or in groups. All the material you're reading now has been updated and rewritten to be relevant today.

I began learning how to write as a reader, then got my master's in creative writing from Manchester Metropolitan University. Sage Hill, Banff Centre for Arts and Creativity with Lisa Moore, Madeline Thien, and Rawi Hage as my teachers, and classes online have taught me more, especially at The Novelry, where I now work as a writing coach with writers from all over the world. I have piles of books about writing all over my house. Some of my favourites are listed at the end.

I'm always a student. While I write this for you, I'm learning, too. As I think about writing and share my ideas with you, it sparks new ideas and shows me new ways to interpret the world and write.

CREATE YOUR WRITING LIFE NOW

To me, it's important that you start to write as frequently as you can, in a consistent way, if possible, as you read this book. As I've mentioned, this book has exercises at the end of each chapter for you. Whether you use the exercises or not, I'd love for you to get words on the page. Writers write. I hope, more than anything, this book encourages you to make time for writing. Use the prompts and suggestions to get words down, if they spark fire in you. Set aside writing time daily, if possible. That's not always possible for me, so don't feel pressured to create an impossible schedule. Just find what works for you.

Perhaps by the final pages of this book, you'll have a book of your own in your hands. But even if you don't, what you will have is more important: you'll have a *writing practice*.

I also want you to read as much as you can. Then read more. I think the best thing you can do for yourself as a writer is to immerse yourself in the brilliant (and not-so-brilliant) work of other writers doing what you want to do. A lot of people who want to write for children or young adults come up to tell me so. They email me or send me a message on social media. At parties, when people ask me what I do, quickly they want to tell me about the idea they have for their own story for kids or teens. What I notice is that a lot of these people haven't had much time to read recently, and they certainly haven't dived into the beautiful ocean of books that are out there for young readers today. It always seems like a missed opportunity. As a writer, I'm rooted in the books I read: they show me what's possible and what's not being done yet.

I don't know what type of reader you are, but I think it's important to make time in the next few weeks to read at least a few books. I have a reading rule, and it's a strict one, which is to read at least fifty pages a day. I've stuck with it all the way through my writing life, and it has served me well. It may be that you don't love adding books into your schedule, it may be that you read voraciously already, or perhaps you're somewhere in between. Some people love to write a reading diary, noting which books they've read. As you read this book, you might want to make your own reading diary as a record of what you love, and also of what you notice as you read.

If I wake in the night, I open my eReader and the quiet light pulls me in. If I'm waiting for something, and no child is dragging at my leg, I take out a book instead of my phone. I set myself reading lists and challenges to keep reading exciting: every October, I read all the way through the Giller Longlist, for example. Perhaps I read everything by one author, or I read only picture books for five days straight.

It may be that you find it helpful to give yourself a challenge to reignite your relationship with reading. And remember, this isn't something you *should* be doing (that word always makes me rebel!), it's something you *could* be doing to get better as a writer.

Your stories matter, your words are important, and this book's job is to give you what you need to create your own writing life, whether that's writing for children or young adults. Ultimately, you'll be writing for yourself. That voice inside you that tells you that you want to write will change who you are in the world—allowing your writing self to spark and create.

PART 1

PREWRITING

1
IDEAS

BEING OPEN TO IDEAS

Apparently, a chance encounter with a little girl in an ice cream store sparked the idea for *Wonder* (by R.J. Palacio). It seems simple—a moment happens, an idea appears, and voilà, a story is born, the book is written, and readers love it. But it doesn't work like that for most writers, and it doesn't work like that for me. In fact, my ideas often start very small: a word, a sentence, half-seen shadows in the dark recesses of my mind, little glimmers and sparks showing themselves before they slip away.

Maybe your ideas walk into your mind as characters, or shimmer as first lines, or you have a big question you want to answer that will become the thematic underpinnings of the story you eventually write. Maybe a setting or a scene appears like a dream. Or you overhear an imaginary line of dialogue. This is what happened for me as the entry point to *Violet and Victor Write the Best-Ever Bookworm Book*, my first published picture book. I "overheard" Violet and Victor arguing with each other as I tucked my kids into bed. Author Anthony Browne has said, "Stories come to me in mysterious ways, more like dreams than reasoned creations."

Many aspiring writers have glimmers of ideas, but before the idea is a possibility, the potential writer has crushed it. They say to themselves: *That's dumb. That's been done before. No one would want to read that. I don't know where to start.*

Perhaps you, too, actually have ideas but you discard them as too silly, too wild, too ridiculous, too *something* to be an actual idea.

The secret is, I think, that no idea is too *anything*. An idea is just that. An idea. Write it down. You can play with it, you can change it, you can look at it from all sorts of different angles, but you have to learn to let it appear on the page and recognize that an idea doesn't need a value judgment, not yet. For now, it just needs to be.

Maybe you don't have any ideas at all. Just an urge to write. That's okay, too. I meet writers all the time who aren't sure what to write about, they just *know* they want to write. I believe a ludicrous theory that ideas are like angels (Gabriel García Márquez said something along those lines that I read years ago, and I love the image). What it means to me is that there are ideas everywhere. Now you just have to learn to be open and ready for them to arrive.

So, think of yourself as a magpie. Take notes of the shiny things that interest you. Write down anything and everything, slight or silly as it may seem. You can use a notebook with a pen, a dictation app in your phone, a file on your computer. I text myself notes (one of my kids has changed my own name in my phone to "Boo Boo Butt," so my texts to myself with my precious ideas are always utterly daft). Hemingway said, "My working habits are simple: long periods of thinking, short periods of writing." So keep in mind that even when you're not writing, you're still thinking, and in this fermentation, an idea can develop.

In the rest of this chapter, we'll explore ways for you to allow your ideas to begin.

Five Tips to Be Open to Ideas

1. Read. We look at this in Chapter 5, but I encourage you to start now.

2. Observe the world, as we'll explore below.

3. Ask yourself the question *what if*. Ask it all the time. What if I had never stood at a train station in Cheltenham and waited for a man called Yann to arrive? What if my little son grew wings and flew away? What if I had a book and everything I wrote in it came true? What if my boss turned into a monster (well, I'm my own boss, but what if your boss, or your friend's boss, or the local high school principal)… Quiet the inner critic that tells you the idea is ridiculous. Just let it have a little room; even put some words on the page.

4. When you're writing for young readers, it's important to be interested in their world as it is *now*. Read the books kids this age read, watch their shows, and try to see why kids like them (a lot of kids' shows are excellent, and some, not so much—same as books). Spend time online and gaming. Yes, that's right, permission to scroll! If you don't have kids in your life, through home or friends or work, then shows and books and gaming are going to be good research ground for you. If you do have kids who you can learn from, listen to them, pay attention to their interests, ask them questions, notice who they are and what matters to them in this world. By increasing your own exposure to the lives of kids in the contemporary world, you open yourself to having ideas.

5. Dig deep into your own past for inspiration.

OBSERVATION

Pay attention to stories you hear and you love. Notice the news and the world as it's happening—perhaps your neighbour is having an affair and you've seen her standing outside furtively upon her phone. You likely don't want to write her story, but it may inspire your own. Perhaps you wonder what it's like for her teenage daughter when it's revealed that the lover is the school principal. How would the teenager in this story navigate the fallout?

Some days, I'm completely immersed in daily life: kids, work, my phone. I forget to pay attention, and then when I go to sit down to write, I'm grasping at air. I have no start points, no moments I want to interrogate with words. Since having children, it's harder to pull back and craft a sentence. Instead, I'm bending over the dishwasher, or trying to check email and sign forms for school and get supper on the table. Afterward, when I'm full of the pleasure or absolute stress that is the day-to-day, I'm too spent to make notes on anything, and I've forgotten to observe *anything*.

But, really, your job as a writer is to pay attention. Notice, as I just did a few minutes ago as I took a writing break, the way a night wind took a confetti of fall leaves, which glinted like coins glittering in the streetlight, as my dog stared inkily at me. Sure, it's overwritten at the moment, but there are verbs and words in there that I know I can use again.

Note details of your ordinary day: you're the only person on the planet to experience that moment the way that you did. Likely you already are somewhat observational, but really pay attention now. Think of the first word that you'd use to describe the weather, say. Then stop and put another word, and then another. Make a sentence and see if it approximates your experience when you read it back. Write down what you overhear. (Creepy, yup, so be discreet! At lunch at McNally Robinson, our beautiful bookstore in Saskatoon, I overheard a woman say to her friend, "He knew something was wrong because of the taste of his tongue." This line bounces with energy and potential, which is all you can ask from an idea at this stage.)

Think about your own interests: what makes you light up? What sparks fire inside you? What do you want to know more about? Often these avenues are the doorways to great ideas. It's another way to observe.

QUIETING THE INNER CRITIC

It doesn't hugely matter at this stage if the idea is good. It matters if it interests you, if, as you write it, you feel energized and excited. And then, as time goes by, that energy will either grow or fizzle out.

In the writing, the idea—that tiny spark—fans and flames. It's really important not to be too hard on yourself or your words at this stage. And that's because at this stage, most of what you write might not be good. That's not my judgment of your work. I might really like what you've written. The person who is judging your work is you, and most writers when they first encounter their own words on the page can be hypercritical. It's like when you hear your own voice in a recording: it doesn't sound the way you want it to. Most of what I write in the first draft is messy and awkward. It doesn't compare to the clean and clear writing that I hope my final draft will be.

I remind myself: The first draft is not the last draft.

And nor should it be. It's okay to make a mess as you write.

It's really important to know that most first drafts have a lot of work to be done on them, and that's part of the process. It's normal, whether you plan the story or book out or you fling words onto the page in a rush, Jackson Pollock style.

Maybe you can write it perfectly the first time. But just in case you read over your words and feel miserable about your failure as a writer, and you chastise yourself for having rubbish ideas, keep in mind that those thoughts are going to extinguish the spark of your idea like a bucket of cold water. This is your Inner Critic. Your job right now is to quiet it.

Tell it: stop.

In my computer are thousands and thousands of words that I've never shared, and likely never will. All of those words have had a reader, an invented character who lurks inside—the Inner Critic. That character can be unkind or rhapsodic, and it reads over your shoulder while you write. I don't always manage to quiet the often cruel reader who I've created and who reads everything I write. But when I notice it, I tell it: stop.

For now, get words on the page. Don't judge yourself, really at all if you can. Learning early on to celebrate your successes as a writer, whether they seem small or are huge, is a useful skill. So, say kind things to your writing self, like: *Well done for sitting down and writing for ten minutes. That's more than yesterday.*

DIGGING DEEP FOR STORIES

Remember your own experiences when you were young. This doesn't mean you'll be writing books about that era (although you might), but it does mean that you're reconnecting with that part of you who was experiencing the world for the first time. Childhood and young adulthood are both so much about those first experiences, which are formative because how we deal with an experience the first time often leads to how we deal with every similar experience after. When we talk about formative years, that's what we mean, and as writers, understanding this is a crucial way to tap into what's important for the readers you're hoping to connect with.

When I remember growing up, I'm in a detached house on Warminster Road, South Norwood, England, feeling like an outsider all the time. That urge to belong is important for all of us, and as a kid who was both insanely sociable and yet constantly reading, I never felt like I fit in. I suspect a lot of other people feel like that, but I didn't know that at the time. I lived with my awkward self, dissembling and trying to be who I thought other people wanted me to be.

I remember going to my grandmother's house and admiring a glass vase where she kept many little books of matches. Behind it, a grape vine trailed up into her conservatory, a place I walked through with my grandfather on our way to his tomato plants.

I remember the first time I kissed a boy. His name was Tim and I'd met him at judo. I remember wanting him to kiss me so much—it would never have crossed my mind that I could have kissed him. And then, when he finally did, it was nothing like what I'd expected. Even thinking back, it makes me cringe: it was a terrible kiss. But it stays there in my memory as an opportunity for a story one day.

I remember the day my parents told me they were separating and the way I felt like I frayed all the way through.

What do you remember?

By remembering your own younger years, you start to notice doors that you haven't opened before. One of those doors could fly open and reveal a whole world of possibility for you as you begin your journey writing for young people.

FREEWRITING: JOY AND FEAR

Freewriting is a technique where you sit and write without stopping. Don't go back over, delete, or fix. Let the words flow. The writing *process* opens up the possibility of a finished written idea. It can be utterly intimidating to "just write," but if you learn to let go and get words down onto the page, it helps you create a foundation of writing *as practice*. You don't need to worry about writing something incredible. Just write to enjoy writing. (It may turn out incredible, that's great. My freewriting always ends up messy and making little sense!)

Often, I start a block of time with a few minutes of freewriting to get going, and that leads me deep into a writing session. As I focus in on the scene I'm writing after a few minutes of freewriting, I might reread each sentence a couple of times before moving on, or pause and go back over a paragraph. But usually, I just write and then go back later editorially.

My partner is a writer, and he does it differently. He pauses at each sentence *as he writes it*. He weighs up every word, editing as he writes. I tell you this because I find it helpful to know that different writers have different ways of being in their own flow space. Mine has a lot to do with the tap of the keys, the exposing of the path through the trees as I walk the words onto the page, the way becoming clear as words fall like leaves around me.

Here are five prompts to free-write with. You can use these and set a timer if you like. Try for ten minutes, write freely, and don't censor or edit yourself.

1. When he looked at me, I knew…
2. He opened the door and then it was too late…
3. There was no way out of the ship…
4. She had to raise her voice…
5. I won't do that ever again…

Use whichever prompt you like for your own work—there are millions out there—and you also have your own prompts all around you. The moment you woke this morning; the thing your friend said; the horrible words you read in the paper; the last thing you said to your loved one; the earthquake that shook the ground in your imagination when you made supper yesterday. Any of the shows, video games, or social media moments you took a look at as you explored the world that young people live in today. The world is full of possible starting points. You will find what works for you, but freewriting can be a good way to get yourself completely out of worrying about whether your idea is any good. (You have no way of knowing if it's a good idea yet, remember. That comes *way* later.)

Learning to play with words while allowing ideas onto the page with no expectation is key to a writing life.

REGULAR WRITING

Time is the greatest thing to happen to ideas. It sorts them for you. Some ideas flicker out and fade as time goes by, and some start a slow burn that grows into a roaring fire. I have to spend some time on the page. I can have ideas as much as I like, but if I'm not regularly writing, those ideas fizzle out, and even ideas that could turn into something amazing vanish forever.

The easiest way to give your notes and sparks time to grow into ideas that could be stories is to spend some time writing in a frequent way. I'd tell you to write every day, but I don't write every day and a lot of people don't have time for that at all. It gets intimidating, impossible, and then no writing happens at all. Instead, think about how you could be writing for a period of time as many of the days of the week as you can. Perhaps you can do as Julia Cameron, the author of forty books, many of them about the creative process, suggests: write morning pages. Take a look at her well-known book *The Artists' Way* for more on this. Maybe you prefer to write once your home is dark and quiet in the evening. Maybe you can take a writing lunch break or a Saturday morning hour once a week.

Whatever you're able to do at this stage is going to help you learn to recognize when you're having an idea. As writing becomes a more regular practice (and please head to the exercises at the end of this chapter), you'll give your fledgling ideas room to grow.

LOST IDEAS

I had a good idea for something I wanted to write a few minutes ago. I was in the bath, looking at a candle, momentarily taking a deep breath. I don't spend a lot of time lying in the bath, looking at candles, letting my mind flow and float, ideas drifting in like multicoloured clouds. In fact, lying-in-the-bath moments are rare. So rare, that I almost didn't get out of the bath to come and write down the magical flowing thought I had.

But I did get out of the bath. Then I realized my computer was downstairs, and I grabbed a towel and padded down, wet feet all over the floor. Yann asked me if I'd seen the letter about phone insurance, and my daughter asked me a question about her homework, so by the time I sat down, the idea was gone.

What I wanted to write about shimmers like a light at the edge of the horizon. A spark. Tempting, glinting, forgotten.

I'm not going to tell you to get a notebook to write down your ideas as they come so that you never forget them. You absolutely can do that; it's a good idea. I'm sure a lot of my ideas would be saved that way. For me, I am not the sort of person who is able to carry around a notebook. I would lose it. I'm the sort of person who has nine different notebooks, each of them started (with pretty pen colours), and none of them finished, and not a single one with a word of fiction inside. I write fiction on my computer, because the flow and the rhythm and the *tappity tap* of the keys help me keep up with the words in my mind.

If only I could remember what they were...

I've had to learn to accept that I can't write down all the ideas I have. Not because I have so many, but because I've taken a life path that means my days are silly-full and it's impossible to hold those bright-light Tinker Bell ideas close. I've lost many more ideas than I've saved. I may never remember the idea I intended to share with you. Instead, I have to let it go. I have to inhabit the one life I get to live, and if I lose an idea, then I let it go.

All this is to say: I think it's important for you to know what sort of person you are when it comes to your ideas. They may be precious coins, shiny and something you cannot leave buried in a treasure box under the sand. You have to dig to find them. Right now. You have to close your office door, or put on headphones, or take a retreat from your kids, or tell your partner that you can't talk about phone insurance right now. (I did tell him that, but it didn't make any difference, mind you.)

Maybe your ideas are so frequent and scattered they're more like the sparks from fireworks. Gorgeous to watch, but not something you have to gather. Mine, I've decided, feel a bit like that to me. When my ideas vanish, I'm sad at the sudden dark, but I'm good to wait for when they happen again.

The ideas that I end up working with are the ideas that come back, over and over. Sometimes in new and unexpected ways. Polly Diamond is an example of this. She started with a name and then continued with me writing in my office at the Saskatoon Public Library, before, after a lot of twists and turns and edits and changes, her book led to me touring the west coast of the US, eating oysters in San Francisco. (Sometimes my job is utterly glamourous and fantastic. Often it looks like me wrapped in a towel, wet feet, kids like pinballs bouncing off the walls, while I try to remember an idea.)

CHAPTER 1 EXERCISES

The following exercises are to help generate ideas. Have fun with them. Commit right here to allowing every idea you have to exist. Forbid yourself from canning anything at this stage: allow the silly and the sublime to come into being.

Practical Task

Decide where you're going to make your notes for ideas. I strongly recommend a software called Dabble. It works beautifully for me. You could have a notebook. Or nine. You could use your phone. Find something that works for you.

What you're aiming for is a space where you have an idea "file." Whether that's on paper or on fancy software, what I'd love is for you to have a place where you can drop yourself a memo/note/line whenever you have ideas.

Writing: 10 Minutes

Write for ten minutes without stopping, judging, or thinking (you can use a timer if you want). Use *one* of the following prompts, if that helps get you started. Or use one of your own.

- the last time I saw my father
- the lake
- family reunion

Likely, the piece of writing will be over for you when you get to the end of this activity. But it may not be. It may spark the path that you travel for the next seven years. You never know where the story you finish and share with the world is going to begin.

Writing: 30 Minutes

Write for thirty minutes recalling a memory when you were either surprised, frightened, or dealing with something you found unfair as a child. If you prefer, you can use a fictionalized character and have this event happen to them currently.

Taking It Further

When you're playful and open, and when you're trying new things, you're giving yourself a new way to view the world, and you're allowing the fizz and bubble of a possible idea to happen. Here are ten ways you can try to generate ideas to finish up this chapter.

1. Work your way through a list of writing prompts, one a day for a week.
2. Take yourself somewhere you've never been and explore it. Make notes.
3. Look for a photograph that means something to you. Write about it.
4. Volunteer with a local organization that you've never heard of before. Make notes.
5. Sit down with a friend and interview them about their life.
6. Look through current or past newspaper headlines and find one that speaks to you. Read as much as you can on that topic. Make notes.
7. List twenty things that you're interested in or that you feel passionate about. Look over your list and see if there's something in there that might work as a story. Explore it.
8. Approach a stranger at a gathering and learn about the work that they do.
9. Go to a gallery and view the work. Do not look at the titles. Give the works your own titles.
10. Take a line from a poem or a book. Use this as a starting point for an idea. What if you change one word? Which word, if changed, would have the most impact?

2
ROOTS

George R.R. Martin says, "A reader lives a thousand lives before he dies." This sums up how I feel about reading: each book gives you an opportunity to inhabit another way of being. As a writer, the opportunity of other books is a deep mine for your creativity. Reading is crucial to my writing life, so I have a long list of titles for you to explore at the back of this book. You absolutely don't have to read all these books, or even most of them. But I do recommend that you read some and that you make reading a key part of your writing life.

In this chapter, we'll look at how to make time for reading and the rules I set for myself to keep reading fun and educative: reading like a writer is a different experience than simply curling up with a book.

MY READING LIFE

One of my favourite photographs is of a child reading. It's a generic picture (Google "child reading" and you'll see something similar). In the specific photograph I love, the child is absolutely absorbed in the pages of a book. Their eyes dance with light and the child's smile is joyful. The photograph energizes me because it reminds me of my own absolute pleasure in reading, and of the power written words have to connect us.

It also reminds me of myself as a kid, because I was absolutely and utterly addicted to reading. I perfected the art of *walking* while holding a book, turning the pages on the long stroll back from the bus stop to my house after school, autumn leaves and misty skies vanishing into the hot California sun beaming on the girls at Sweet Valley High, say. I was dedicated to making sure I used every opportunity to immerse myself in books. I read and still read constantly, and that's not hyperbole. As a teenager, I could slot a book between the glass exterior of the shower and the sink cupboard, so I slid books in there, got out wet to turn the page, then went back in to read *while I was showering*. Late at night, I'd angle the pages so the light from the walkway would illuminate them, squinting my eyes so I could disappear into the worlds offered by the authors, staying up way past bedtime.

I was lucky, too, that my parents read to me. I particularly remember my father reading to me from a book called *Elidor*. His low rumbling voice as I drifted off, the fantastical land of Alan Garner (shortlisted for the Booker Prize in 2022, which shows how magnificently long his writing career has been), transporting me nearly forty years ago. My mum regularly took me and my siblings to the library in South Norwood, a suburb of London where I grew up. The library had windows that looked out onto the end of the high street, a slightly run-down and ratty part of the city. Inside, books towered over us, enticing us with their promises.

The world of books for children and young adults was nothing like it is now, but I was deeply grateful for authors who were opening doors I would later travel through as a writer. Books like *Are You There God? It's Me, Margaret*, *Beezus and Ramona*, *The Tesseract*, *Anne Frank: The Diary of a Young Girl*, and many others laid a foundation. Quickly, I exhausted the books directed toward my age group. Dick and Jane drove me bananas and I hankered for books that would satisfy my curiosity. I worked my way through my mum's bookshelves, disappearing into *Clan of the Cave Bear* and then everything by Penelope Lively, who I barely understood, but who I loved.

As you're probably gathering, I'm an indiscriminate reader (you picked that up when I mentioned Sweet Valley High, right?). My bedside table now has a pile of eclectic books upon it, ranging from current shortlisted books for major prizes, to the latest Saskatchewan publications, to outstanding young adult, like *Firekeeper's Daughter* by Angeline Boulley, which I'll come back to. I have books about writing, like *Story Genius* by Lisa Cron or *How to Tell a Story* compiled by The Moth (my favourite podcast), and then magazines (*The New Yorker*, *The Atlantic*, *Writer's Digest*), a crime novel (I adore Tana French), and kids' book series I'm reading with my children: The School for Good and Evil, Archie Comics, and The Bolds, alongside a selection of graphic novels by David A. Robertson. I read cereal packets, shampoo bottles, and everything I can on creating online content because I co-founded and now help run a non-profit website called OneSmallStep.com, which makes it easy for people in Saskatoon to discover the work of local charities by having them all in one place for free.

READING LIKE A WRITER

In a world with AI-generated text available to all of us as writers if we choose to use it, the art of reading becomes even more important. Knowing *how* you want words to sound, knowing what works for *you*, helps you hone a text as you craft. The more you read, the more you'll hone that inner ear.

Interestingly, the first thing I do to get myself into a writing frame of mind is read. Robert Louis Stevenson wrote, "I kept always two books in my pocket, one to read, one to write in." This matches with my writing life: as I read, ideas spark. To me, every book is a teacher. Each and every book—even the terrible ones—can teach you something about writing: how to do it, how *not* to do it, how someone else has done it, how you could do it.

When you're reading like a writer, you are both enjoying the book you're reading and you're thinking about it as a teacher *itself*. It's a mindset to get into that has helped me through the years to become a better writer overall (I think!). When I'm reading, I notice what I love. I highlight sentences that I admire, reading them over carefully and letting them swell in my mouth. I notice, too, what I don't like. The moments I get lost or bored help me pay attention to the types of stories I want to write. Above all, I tune in to the books that pull me to them. Which books do you love? What do you select at the bookstore?

As you read, explicitly thinking as a writer, I want you to try these two steps:

1. **Try to push yourself outside of your comfort zone.** Challenge yourself to read books you wouldn't normally pick up. Read picture books and YA novels, read self-help and poetry. Try science fiction (*please* pick up a book by N.K. Jemisin), try grim realism, *try it all.* The reason for this is that a lot of us get stuck in a bit of a reading rut in our lives. But this book aims to help you become the writer you want to be. To do that, I want you to become a little more playful and open to possibility. A great way to do this is to read outside of what you have mainly read up until now, no matter how far along the writing journey you are. You can always put down a book you don't love once you've tried it out. When I started reading lots of chapter books, I realized how much I loved them: sparks flew to me from those books that I then wanted to emulate in my own writing. I want this experience for you.

2. **Pay attention to the books you love most.** Once you've expanded your reading options, you can fully notice what you most enjoy as a reader. I find a huge correlation between this and what you most want to write. If you're pulled over and over to picture books, then likely that's the type of book you want to write

> next. This works both ways—if you're trying to write something that you don't love to read, you could ask yourself why. I love crime fiction, and have won an award for writing crime fiction, but it's taken me years to recognize that I perhaps want to write more of it. I spent weeks over the summer reading everything by Tana French and saw that I was interested as a writer in understanding the psychological impact of a crime on people around the victim. In my YA novel, *The Death of Us*, which I wrote years ago, I followed this passion, and in the novel I'm writing now, I find myself fizzing with excitement when I think about the mystery and murder aspects of the story.

THE READING LISTS

As you're thinking about these two important tasks, I have some reading lists for you in the section called Places to Go at the end of this book. The first is a list of picture books to get you excited. The next is a list of chapter books for different ages, and then I move into a reading list of some terrific middle grade and young adult novels, series, and graphic novels. The last three lists I co-compiled with Laura Backes.

As you're exploring these lists, you're welcome to cross out the books as you read them, make notes on the list, and connect with me any time to tell me which books you've enjoyed. I want you to notice what you love, and notice what doesn't work for you. That's why I've left space at the end of each list for you to add your own books.

Sometimes I've recommended reading any and all of a series, sometimes I've highlighted a particular book, and sometimes I've left the choice up to you. While most of the books are recent titles (published in the last fifteen years or so), I've put in some classic books that are popular with readers today because they have timeless characters, plots, or illustrations. They're worth studying, not just for reading pleasure but because they have influenced modern books.

Some of these older books don't quite fit all the rules of writing for young readers, particularly the age of the characters. You'll also notice, especially as you get to the books for older readers, that the books aren't separated by genre. Explore plots and genres that you might not otherwise read, or those that you think you may not like. You might realize that you really want to write something you've never even considered.

I've added a list of books about writing that I love, and some great places online for you to read more about writing and creating good habits (like the reading rule we're about to make together!).

Remember, these book lists are just ideas for you to explore. Please don't be daunted by the lengths of the lists, and please let me know if you find a book that you love that's not on here so I can read it! I've added some extra Canadian content, and every month I share books I love on CTV, with lots of Saskatchewan authors being my focus. So, take a look, read some, and then pick.

As you read, note what you like and what you don't: if you're making a reading diary, it might be a good place for this work. You could even copy out the first page and see how the writer works—this is a tip from Laura, and it's very helpful because as you copy out the work of other writers, you see the cadence of their voice, the structure of their sentences, and how they brought their characters to life on the page. This doesn't change your voice, just deepens your understanding of how the book you're reading has come into being.

CHAPTER 2 EXERCISES

Practical Task

I want you to give yourself a reading rule. Perhaps you want to read for thirty minutes a day/every second day. Perhaps you want to read a picture book a day or a middle grade novel a week. Perhaps you want to follow my fifty-pages-a-day rule. Whatever your rule, commit to it. If after a few weeks, you're not achieving it, change the rule until it's something you can incorporate into your life.

Hopefully, it's something you'll take with you long after you've finished this book. I guarantee it'll make you a better writer, and it will also help you bring and keep reading in your life—something many people want to do but never quite get around to.

Writing: 10 Minutes

Find a photograph. It can be a stock photo. It can be a photograph of your favourite place. It can be a photo of someone you love (or dislike!). Take one minute just to look at the photograph.

Set a timer and free-write for ten minutes without worrying about whether you're getting it wrong or right. Put words onto the page.

Writing: 30 Minutes

The moments when children fall asleep when they're young, leaving their parents or caregiver behind, are big in their lives. Some children sleep safely in their beds. Some deal with real or imagined terrors. Some wake up to calm and many wake up to stress and the day-to-day rumble of whichever adults are in their lives. It's all fodder for storytelling.

Have you remembered the passage of time and the amount of time that sleep takes and plays into our lives? Write for 30 minutes about nighttime. See where it takes you: portals, dreamworlds, the sweet kiss of goodnight... or who knows? Only you can tell!

Taking It Further

One wonderful place to explore in your reading is the world of fairy tales, folktales, and myth. These foundational stories remind us of our own childhoods and resonate anew as we start thinking about the stories we want to write. Choose at least one fairy tale, folktale, or myth that you loved as a child and read it over. Make some notes on what you felt as a reader. Now try to write your own. Remember, you can't get this wrong...

3

The OPTIONS *for* WRITING *for* YOUNG READERS: OVERVIEW

PUBLISHING YOUR BOOK FOR YOUNG READERS

We all want to share our stories. That's human, whether we're a writer or not. For some writers, publishing is their north star. I know this, because for years it was my *only* "why."

One afternoon, when I was 19, I was on a boat adrift in the waters between islands in Indonesia (which turned into its own adventure). Onboard were other travellers. One was an older man and for some reason, likely my need for validation, I showed him the story I was writing. It was called *All the Different Blues*, and it was about a boy who fished for shades of blue in the ocean.

"Yeah, it's okay," the man said. He handed back my pages. "I don't really get it. Like, yeah." He turned to the vast actual blue and my heart diminished. Hot with shame, I folded up my words, mumbled something, and put everything into my backpack. The sun was shining, the air was sweet, the water stretched for miles in every direction, and I was aching. If this man didn't value my writing, then how could *I*?

The answer appeared to me: I needed to get *published*.

That would show the man that I was a real writer. I wanted my writing to be good enough in someone else's eyes. For a long time, that need for validation tugged me along.

I tell you this not because I'm comfortable sharing my craven desires, but because I want you to know that wanting to be published is valid. But, although sharing work with other people can be part of a writing life, it's not the key.

The key to a writing life is listening to *yourself*. When you learn to listen to what you're truly wanting to say, when you learn to trust your judgment on the page, you're living the writing life you most want. I know this because I've been living a writing life for a long time and I know that when I value the words I've written, then the response from the world stops being the motivator. Learning to listen to what you love and what you don't about your writing is how you flourish. The sparks that flare in the dark become something that matters to *you*. Other people don't get to decide for you if you're good enough as a writer. You decide when you're satisfied with your words. Now that you're a writer for young readers, the words of Madeleine L'Engle could be your north star. She wrote, "You have to write the book that wants to be written. And if the book will be too difficult for grown-ups, then you write it for children." Publishing is wonderful and fun, and I hope your book/s get published. But writing because the book *wants to be written*, and you're the only person who can write it, is a far more powerful fuel.

SHOULD YOU WRITE THIS STORY?

While, as authors, we want to tell stories, there are some considerations before we launch forth. It's crucial to think about cultural appropriation, diversity in publishing, and the notion that anyone can write whatever they want.

Over the last several years, it's become visible in the dominant white culture that there hasn't been space in the world of published books for diverse writers or diverse stories. This is changing, but very slowly. Finally, as readers, we're able to find books by a greater range of authors, sharing perspectives and experiences through story that illuminate worlds and lives that have been oppressed or forced out of sight. There is still a lot of work to be done on the part of the industry. Throughout the years of our reading lives, a lot of the stories have been from the perspective of writers who have no experience of the lives of the characters they write about. Bookshelves full of books by authors who have believed they have the right to any story, a colonial approach, leads to stories that stereotype and spread misinformation.

Cultural appropriation happens when we take a story from a culture that's not our own, with no respect for that culture or understanding of difference. Often writers don't intend to do any harm, but that's not an excuse. It's important to be rigorous with yourself at the start of your project as to whether the story you want to write is yours to tell. While this doesn't mean that you can only write from your lived experience, it does mean that you have an opportunity to pause before you assume you have the right to plunder whichever story you want.

The first question for me here is: where does that belief come from?

Writers who believe they own any story they want, and the world is theirs for the taking as a creator, need to consider if this is an entitled viewpoint. And untrue. Each of us has a wonderful and unique angle from which we see the world, and from where we experience it. Thousands of stories are in our own repertoire, stories that only we are able to tell.

If you do think that you want to write from the perspectives of historically and currently marginalized populations, but you are not from this group and these are not your own stories, then I recommend you pause.

I always ask myself what it is about the story or character that pulls me to it. What's my connection, if any, and what connections do I have to other stories that only I can tell? Would those stories be a more powerful place to explore?

By writing this story, do I possibly take away from an author who has lived experience and cultural perspectives that I don't? If so, why am I wanting to write this? What will it teach me *and others*? Or will it take away? Does my own cultural identity, lack of experience, or understanding, despite research and best attempts, mean this story will perpetuate stereotypes or misunderstandings, or trigger trauma?

What connections do I have to people in the community I want to write about who might be able to read my work to ensure it is truthful, accurate, and respectful? Am I well poised to listen to those responses? Do I intend to pay for consultation? Do I listen to stories or read the work of writers from this community? Do I bring my point of view to another culture without being curious about what I don't know? Are there elements I may never be able to know or understand, and how will my biases perpetuate stereotypes?

And then I sit with this last thought for a bit: Will I be taking or giving when I commence this project?

These questions can help you find a path that is best for your potential readers, for the story you want to explore, and for your writing. At this point, I want to direct you to a website where you can take classes, learn, explore, and interrogate your work and thoughts. The organization is called Writing the Other and the link is at the end of this book.

THINKING ABOUT YOUR BOOK FOR YOUNG READERS

As you begin the work of writing, being honest with yourself about whether you're writing a book for others or if you're writing it for yourself is useful. There's not a right answer here: it's not that one version is better, it's that one is going to be more honest for you.

If you want to write a book for others, then you need to be clear with yourself that there are conventions and expectations along that path. This is a career option, and you'll need to do many things as well as write the book. You have to become an author *in* the world. That can look like a self-published author running your own business, perhaps making it huge online, or it can look like being a traditionally published author with a publishing house supporting your book. When we get to the last part of this book, we'll look into ways you can make your work ready for the world, and where you might want to send it. I'll share with you everything I know and have learned about the industry to help you find a home for your work.

For now, take time to learn about the different age groups and audiences for books for young readers. It will help you as you decide where to position your book in the world.

Maybe you want to write a book only for you. If this is your path, you have much more freedom. Your finished book may never have commercial value or be a consumer product, but it will teach you things you never knew before and create surprising connections and beauty in your life, fulfilling you creatively. (Honestly, this is the case whether you end up publishing or not!)

Keep in mind, as you move forward with writing, that you can start a book for yourself and then decide later that you might want to share it with the world. But be careful that the judgment of others isn't what determines the worth of your writing. I often send work out for other people to validate too early. I struggle to resist that impulse to have someone else tell me that my work is "worth it." I have to fight that urge that first showed up so vividly on that boat in Indonesia, years ago.

Whether the book you're writing is for you, for others, or you're not sure yet, learning the many conventions for books for young readers is extremely useful for you as you shape your work. It shows you the range and possibility out there for you to try.

The publishing industry has clear expectations for the books they consider and publish for different audiences (different age groups). I find the word *audience* helpful because it helps you not get mixed up with the *genre* of the book (whether the book is science fiction, historical, crime, romance, etc.). YA sci-fi, for example, shows you the age of the audience—young adult—and the genre—science fiction.

So, the audience refers specifically to the approximate age of your potential readers.

There are a lot of rules for writing for young readers, and when you understand those rules you can use them as parameters for what you're intending to do. Some stories I've tried to write work better when I tried them for a different age group. We'll start with some broad rules, before we hone in on audiences any further.

GOOD INITIAL RULES WHEN WRITING FOR YOUNG READERS

1. **Don't moralize or preach.** Children are smarter than many adults give them credit for, and they'll see right through your attempts to lecture them in your book. Home and school are full of rules. When they read, they want to live other lives, have fun, escape. All the things you want when you read a good book, in fact.

2. **Children like to read about other children.** If you're writing a story about a fifty-year-old, you may be writing a book for adults. There are lots of books for children with adult characters, but take note of how those adult characters actually end up being young at heart if not young in age (I'm thinking *Mr. Popper's Penguins*).

3. **Be wary of stereotypes, especially those that are no longer contemporary**. For many kids the current family structure is very different from how it may have been when you were growing up. If you write about Mommy baking in the kitchen and Daddy rushing off to the office, watch for stereotyping that doesn't speak to a contemporary audience.

4. **Think about the time you're setting the book in**. Just because you grew up in the '70s, '50s, '80s, '60s, '90s, '40s, your readers are growing up *now*. Unless your story has a compelling reason to be set in a different decade, pause to think why you're not writing in a contemporary context.

5. **Don't make the mistake of thinking writing for children is easy**. Early Reader *Biscuit* by Alyssa Satin Capucilli, illustrated by Pat Schories, has very few words.

   Go to bed, Biscuit.
   Woof, woof.
   Biscuit wants a drink.

   To write this simply about something that speaks to a child is so much more difficult than most people realize. The repetition, placed so that children learn to read while thrilling at the story, is extremely challenging. The art is to make it look easy, without a young reader being aware of the effort the writer put in.

A NOTE ON THE RULES

If you search online you'll find lots of sites that give word counts, terminology, and rules for writing different formats for children. You'll notice site-to-site variations.

Partly this is because different publishers may have different criteria for the books on their list. And partly because some 11-year-olds are reading adult novels with gusto, others are only just finishing up with picture books. When the delineation of the different categories of books blur, don't let it worry you. These conventions aren't one size fits all—kids are, after all, unique, which is one of the many things that makes writing for young readers so fun.

Also, for every rule and convention, there are authors and books that blow those up. Having the information doesn't make you beholden to how it's been done before. My novel, *Life on the Refrigerator Door*, is too short for any convention, for example. I wrote it because I was interested in what people could see about the relationship between two characters with very few words: the structure and length of the story served the book I wanted to write, so the novel is extremely short.

Finally, with digital and self-publishing growing ever popular, there are all sorts of other options. Stay open to what's out there and see.

FINDING YOUR POSSIBLE AUDIENCE

The books you love to read are a huge clue to the type of book you might want to write.

As *you* read, think about which sort of books you already understand well. Then head out to the library or the bookstore and start reading books in the other categories (using the lists at the back) so you know what's possible for *you* as an author. I can describe the different types of audiences, but until you read a few of each type of book, it's hard to contextualize.

If you read picture book after picture book with pleasure, you'll probably find joy in writing them. If middle grade novels bore you, then you probably aren't suited to writing middle grade at this time in your life. As you read the various books for young readers, listen to your instincts. Don't judge yourself or be frustrated that you don't love one type of book. Let your instincts guide you and discover which books you most like to read. It'll be your first big hint as to what sort of book you might write next. And if you love them all and, like me, you find yourself reading eclectically for all age groups, then there's no reason you can't write for more than one audience. I do it all the time.

The next way to find your voice as a children's author is to start writing. Notice as you write what sort of age your characters tend to be. If you naturally want to write about 16-year-olds, chances are you're writing YA. If, instead, your main character is 9 or 10, you're probably writing a chapter book or very early middle grade novel. So, as you do the prewriting exercises, pay attention to where your heart takes you.

CHAPTER 3 EXERCISES

Practical Task

Carve out a space where you can read and write. My space, as we explore in Chapter 6, looks like headphones: it requires a playlist and very little else. So, make a playlist if you're like me, but don't if you find that distracting. Maybe you need a simple, clear desk in your home where you can sit; or a comfy chair in the corner of a room. Could you select a local cafe and align when you can go there with your work/family life?

Every book you've ever read is by someone who has had to carve out time and space to write it. You can do this, too.

Writing: 10 Minutes

Free-write for ten minutes. Use this starting line: *(Name) could not stop…*

Writing: 30 Minutes

Use the topic *The first time I…(or The first time they/he/she…)*. This prompt is so rich for authors for young readers—being a kid is about experiencing life for the first time!

Which age did you choose for the person you wrote about? Pay attention to this because it might be a clue to the age group you'd like to write for. Are you writing about younger or older children? In the next two chapters we dive deeper into the different options for young readers so you can learn how to spark your creativity.

Taking It Further

All these options will help you get to know yourself as a writer: what type of books for young readers might you write?

1. Draw a bubble and inside it write the words *My life at age (choose an age)*. Connected to this bubble, draw other smaller bubbles. Fill them with memories from the age you chose.

2. Next, look through the reading list at the end of this book and notice which books you've most enjoyed or you're most drawn to. Is there a commonality? What could you write that was about the same thing while being extremely different? Make some notes on this.

3. Finally, read over a book, story, or notes you've written in the past (these can be something you've free-written in an earlier exercise or something that's been sitting in a drawer for years). Try to do this as a *reader* and see what you most love about your writing. Be kind to yourself and see what sparks your imagination. Hold onto that feeling and see whether there might be an idea for a *new* book or story. I'm not suggesting you go back to an old project, although you can; my suggestion is that you pay attention to some of the elements that sparked your excitement.

   Do you love stories set in schools? Or animal characters, for example? Where does this take you next as a writer?

4

The OPTIONS *for* WRITING *for* YOUNG READERS:

Specifics for PICTURE BOOKS *and* CHAPTER BOOKS

FROM PICTURE BOOKS TO CHAPTER BOOKS

When I began Polly Diamond, which is now a chapter book series with Chronicle Books, it started as a picture book. It was called *Polly Diamond Writes to the Moon.* I loved the title and titles are often where my ideas begin. I rewrote it lots of times as a picture book. I read it out loud. I made a dummy picture book, which we'll look into later. But somehow the book didn't do what I wanted it to do, and when I shared it with an editor, it didn't work for her either. I put it to one side.

Around this time, I became a mother. I say that like it was a small shift, but it wasn't. It transformed my relationship with writing because suddenly my time was consumed by family life. My partner and I quickly went on to have three more children, and by the time my daughter—my second child—was 7, she was able to pick up the brand-new hardback edition of *Polly Diamond and the Magic Book*: my chapter book. That sounds like a swift and easy journey—as if I flipped my picture book into a chapter book and suddenly it was published. I hope you noticed the seven-year gap between those two events!

Time and becoming a parent changed my relationship with Polly. As did my knowledge of the different types of books out there in the world for young readers, which gave me the opportunity to try Polly Diamond in a different format. The writing process shifted when I wrote Polly aged at around 8 years old—in one of the many attempts to tell her story—she started to become real on the page. The book unlocked for me. Her character was solidified, and she was in a narrative that began to work.

How did Polly's age make a difference to how the book worked? Let me explain. Books for young readers are centred around the ages of their characters, as we've briefly touched on before. Kids, naturally, want to read about other kids, and they want to read about kids who they are interested in. The same thing happens on the playground. Often, kids want to read about kids their own age or slightly older, the same as they want to play with other kids their own age or slightly older. They deem books with younger kids as central characters to be babyish. If you have kids in your life, you'll notice that younger children are "too little" for them (which can be very cute when they're only a few months older themselves).

Understanding this notion of *character age* helps make the morass of rules in the industry far easier to navigate.

That means the type of book you're writing for young readers depends on the approximate age of your main character and the challenges that character is experiencing. Keeping this in mind as we go into the details of how to write for young readers is going to help, lots. We'll start with books for the youngest readers and work our way up from there.

While I think that taking a little bit more time to understand the different types of books for kids, and then reading some of them, is the most helpful next step for you as a writer, if you're feeling ready to write your book, then do! Remember the wise words of Maurice Sendak: "I don't write for children. I write. And somebody says, that's for children." At the heart of your writing is the urge to create a story, the marketing and placing of your book will come later.

PICTURE BOOKS: ALL TYPES

A picture book is any book that is predominantly illustrated. Including a subcategory known as board books, picture books use illustration to tell the story as well as enhance the text.

Board Books

These are aimed at newborns to kids aged around 3. Typically, board books are 10 to 16 pages with little or no text. Often these are made by authors who've got a proven track record of connecting with very young children and their caregivers, like Richard Van Camp, who has published many beautiful books for little ones.

Sometimes books that were not originally published as board books are so successful that publishers bring out the story as a board book—think *Where Is the Green Sheep* or *Jamberry*.

Many board books originate with the publisher and are written in-house (by someone working at the publishing house). These are often high concept (like *That's Not My Kitten / That's Not My Princess / That's Not My Train*). The concept is more important than the actual text and often the writer's name isn't even on the book.

Emotions and faces and generally other babies are riveting for tiny children, and so you'll see many board books with baby faces.

Authors who write unique board books have to be very talented with language. The inimitable Sandra Boynton is able to be funny, smart, and yet very simple with her wording. She veers from the humorous to the tender with ease. Small children love her work. So do I.

Picture Books, General

Picture books are for readers aged 3 to around 8. The adult reader who is reading the book is also the audience. The illustrations add richness and storytelling elements to the reading experience.

Picture books can be fiction or non-fiction and they're conventionally 32 or 48 pages long. These specific numbers are to do with how books are printed. Usually they're no longer than 1,500 words. Most aren't anywhere near as long as that. A classic text like *Where the Wild Things Are* has 338 words.

For those of you who have to get kids to bed, you'll understand why brevity in a picture book is valued. Reading aloud when kids are overtired can be challenging, especially if you're tired yourself. If the manuscript is overly long, every extra word drags when you're trying to get kids to settle. At least, that's my theory. The length is also to do with the kids themselves, too, helping them stay focused and immersed. Many if not most picture books now run under 1,000 words, and shorter is often better.

As you read more picture books, you'll notice that they're split into books for younger children (ages 3–5) and older (ages 5–8). Picture books for young readers are very short in terms of text, preferably less than 500 or 600 words. *Penguin* by Polly Dunbar is a lovely example of this. So is *Goodnight Moon* by Margaret Wise Brown. Picture books for older readers can go up to 1,500 words, but even for older readers, trying to stay under 1,000 words is more appealing for publishers. (And for readers!)

A NOTE ON RHYME

A lot of writers believe that if they want to write a picture book, they have to write it in rhyme. As you read more picture books, you'll see how many aren't rhyming and you'll take that pressure off yourself.

If you want to work with rhyme, you need to be able to hear the words in your head like music. The best way to do this is to read your work aloud. And to then get someone else to read it aloud afterward to make sure you aren't manipulating the syntax. I often read my writing out loud to myself, even though I don't use rhyme, as it's a helpful editorial tool (which we'll look at later). But if rhyme speaks to you, reading out loud is essential. Also, I suggest that you read poetry and plays to get a sense of how other great writers have mastered the art of the sound of words. Think about the structure of the rhyme you want to use—learning about meter and poetics will well serve any rhymers.

The next step with rhyme is to write and rewrite to get the words perfectly placed on the page. Often, the temptation is to make the line move itself around to fit the rhyme, which is called forced rhyme. Here's an example:

One rainy, wet and yucky day
Becky Lane went outside to play
She wore her shiny boots and bestest hat
And kissed right on the nose the cat

See how I'm introducing an unnecessary element (the cat isn't important for the story) and forcing the line so that cat falls as the last syllable—*kissed the cat on the nose* would be far more natural but wouldn't rhyme.

Remember, you don't have to use rhyme at all to write a beautiful book for young readers: it's just there as an option if it serves your story best.

A NOTE ON ILLUSTRATION

If you're an author/illustrator, like Sandra Boynton or Anthony Browne, you'll be the one illustrating your picture book. As he says, "The illustrations in picture books are the first paintings most children see, and because of that, they are incredibly important. What we see and share at that age stays with us for life." If you have the talent for illustration, when you submit your picture book to publishers, you'll send in two or three finished illustrations along with a visual storyboard for the book as well as your text.

Don't panic. If you can't illustrate to save your life (like me), then your publisher will select your illustrator if you publish along the traditional route.

What? I hear you ask. *The publisher selects the illustrator?!*

Yes, publishers want to pair the illustrator with the author. Picture books are expensive to produce, and any publisher who specializes in picture books will have a bank of eager and talented illustrators they know and trust.

This doesn't mean that you shouldn't think about illustration at all—as the writer, you need to leave room for the illustrator's imagination, and sometimes you'll annotate your text with an art note. But don't fill the page with these art notes if you intend to seek traditional publication. You'll have to trust your publisher and the illustrator to work with limited input.

What? I hear you ask again. *You don't get any say in your illustrations?*

The illustrator actually often needs the freedom to be creative without the author hovering over them. Little, Brown Books for Young Readers asked for my opinion on the types of illustration I liked for my Violet and Victor books. After we talked for a bit, they presented Bethanie Murguia as a possible illustrator. I loved her work and reached out to say hi to her on social media. A call from my editor in New York ensued: "Remember, Alice, we're the ones who communicate with your illustrator."

I quietly let Bethanie do her amazing work, and she did a stunning job. *Without* me, but using my words. The publisher and the illustrator are very much on the same team, but as the writer, unless you have talent for the visual, it's important to allow the artist room to do justice to your work.

If this sounds less than ideal for your vision for your book, remember, you can self-publish. If you do that, you select your illustrator and work closely with them to create the images. What that relationship looks like is up to you both.

THE CHALLENGES AND OPPORTUNITIES OF PICTURE BOOKS

Think of picture books as a playground and of your readers as little ones learning to play. Nothing, it seems to me, is so tricky and so fun to write as an entire story in less than 1,000 words (preferably closer to 500 words). Emily Keyes, a literary agent, has said, "I think the shorter the book, the more each word matters, so the degree of difficulty actually goes up." And I agree. My first published picture book (notice, I don't say the first one I wrote because I wrote at least thirty before that) is 675 words long, and I rewrote it over 300 times. Getting the right words to tell the story was hard. The length is both a challenge and an opportunity: it's a chance for you to hone each phrase and meditate on each word.

Not only do you have the word count challenge, you also have the format to consider. Especially as you begin in the world of printed picture books, aiming for 32 pages as your format is a helpful start. Most publishers prefer this for new authors.

The first couple of pages are used for titles and dedications and the last page often has an illustration upon it or remains blank. Assume that you have 28 pages for your storytelling, which means that the picture book becomes 14 double-page spreads—or 14 scenes, each leading from one to the next. I picture these as stairs in my mind, with 14 steps. As you'll see when you read picture books, there is a range of average words per page, so notice what you prefer as a reader. Do you like the denser pages with lots of words? Or room for air and illustration? Notice, too, that sometimes spreads have no words at all: how does that feel for you as you read?

Page breaks themselves are important in the narrative of a picture book, and as you play with each step (or double-page spread), you can think about how the space between the pages creates narrative movement.

The next challenge/opportunity is the double audience for picture books. Yes, you're writing for the child reader. That little person has their own needs. They are being introduced to stories and language and they are full of questions. They need the story read over and over again.

But you're also writing for the adult reader, a person who is introducing the child to language, a person who wants to sound good when they read the book out loud, a person who wants to enjoy the story just as much on the thousandth read through! (See now why every word matters?)

Two very different picture books show how authors can approach these challenges: *On the Trapline* by David A. Robertson and *The Most Magnificent Thing* by Ashley Spires.

Looking at both of these will show you opportunities to expand your own picture book because you'll see how the illustrations and the stories marry.

David's TD Canadian Children's Literature Award–winning picture book takes the reader on a journey of a character exploring heritage and cultural identity with gorgeous illustration and fine language. A boy and his moshom travel together to Moshom's trapline. The first thing you're likely to notice is that the book uses more than 32 pages, and when you read it you'll see why. David is a well-established writer and so when he writes a book that needs more pages, publishers are willing to explore that option.

David artfully navigates the relationship between character and history so that you know what this book is about from the very first line. This biographical storyline resonates on many levels through language and experience: there's very much a story for young readers and a story happening for adults here. Take time to see how many words he has on each page, and how the narrative and illustrations work together to create beauty and movement.

In *The Most Magnificent Thing* by Ashley Spires, the main character gets frustrated easily (my kids recognize both themselves and me in her!). She really wants to make the most magnificent thing, and yet that doesn't quite work out. This character-driven story follows the conventions of a 32-page picture book, filling the hearts of readers with character, plot, and an adorable doggie! The girl is never named, making her more of a character that all kids can relate to, and yet her personality shines. Notice that Ashley illustrates her own work, and that Dave works with the phenomenally talented Julie Flett.

Both authors use page breaks to make the text compelling. This line is how one double-page spread ends in *The Most Magnificent Thing*:

> *The afternoon fades into evening. Finally, she finishes. She alerts her assistant.*

This type of break makes a young reader want to turn the page to see what happens next.

As you spend time with these two books, think about how they work for you, and what you want to do yourself on the page. Notice how the authors have navigated the challenges and opportunities of picture books and used the conventions to tell incredible stories.

EASY READERS

Sometimes called early readers, these are for readers aged 4 to 8—kindergarten through to second grade. They are written for children who are starting to read alone for the first time. Typically, these books aren't longer than five short chapters. Words used often follow guidelines for early readers, focusing on language that kids will be learning at this stage. These books are often very repetitive and can be anything from 100 words to 2,000 words long, spread over 32 to 64 pages; as you'll see, these pages are smaller than in a traditional picture book and more text heavy. Often these books are highly illustrated, but the text stands alone, which means that you as the writer focus on the action, the character, and the plot, letting the description come through in the images.

Most publishers for young readers have their own series of these types of books, and they are often levelled, which means they are defined by the *level* that the young reader is at as a reader: kids at school are often aware of their reading level and they work with their teacher or caregiver to read through the books in one level before moving into the next one. You'll see these books described as Level One, say, or Level A. The simpler levels often have one syllable words and very short repetitive sentences, and then they become slightly more complex as the levels rise (and the reader grows in confidence and ability).

The I Can Read! books, especially the Frog and Toad series by Arnold Lobel, the Magic School Bus First Readers by Joanna Cole, and the Elephant and Piggie series by Mo Willems are great to read to explore this category. Often, these books are written by authors who are already established, or the books are created in-house (by the publishing team). They are a harder market to break into, in my experience. But, if you have a lot of knowledge about reading levels, this might be a wonderful space for you to write in.

CHAPTER BOOKS

These are aimed at readers ages 5 to 9 or 7 to 10, and they're in the 5,000 (younger) to 15,000 (older) word count range. They are split into about 8 chapters to about 14. They are plot heavy: think Captain Underpants, Clementine, or *Dragon Masters*.

Chapter books are for readers who are starting to read entire books on their own. Remember how excited you were the first times you read *whole* books? Remember the worlds you were transported to and how thrilling it was to be able to dive into a book *all by yourself*?

Illustrations supplement the plot, but are not essential, often depicting scenes as they are written, giving visual clues as readers navigate the story. Helping readers *read*.

Chapter books tend to feature strong characters, with clear storylines moving from point A to point B. Too much backstory or confusing subplots are challenging for readers of this age group, although there may be a simple subplot. Normally there's a problem to be solved. It gets solved. The character grows and changes. It's common that the character is a kid or an animal with a lot of childlike qualities. The character solves their own problems and doesn't have an adult fix the world for them. As you read chapter books, notice how these conventions play out on the page and think about the age of the readers and why these books are the way they are.

Polly Diamond

Polly Diamond and the Magic Book has short chapters—about 500 words each—and is about 8,000 words long. In the opening, Polly Diamond receives a blank book. Everything she writes in the book comes true. Now, if only she'd stop making mistakes in her writing!

Hopefully, the book appeals to teachers because it follows the creative writing curriculum for Polly's age group—aged 7 plus. But more importantly, hopefully it appeals to kids because Polly is endlessly getting into trouble. Accidentally.

For me, the story has a strong character with strong storytelling—both useful for young readers as they become readers on their own for the first time.

Here's the opening sequence:

One—

Today something amazing is going to happen.

Amazing things always happen in threes.

Day One: On Friday, my teacher, Ms. Hairball, told me my color poem was fantastic.

Day Two: On Saturday, my pet rock, Stoneface, smiled at me. I saw him! I swear!

Today is Sunday. Day Three.

So yes. Today is going to be amazing. Super-fantastic.

Notice how the text is written simply and (hopefully) clearly, and the ideas of the story are presented right away. Readers of these sorts of books are still learning narrative conventions, and so keeping the story strong and focused is key. When you write your chapter book, you need to dive right into the story and the characters and not spend too long on description or backstory, especially at the start.

Some of my favourite chapter books are in the Clementine series by Sara Pennypacker. This series is an example of a strong character with great storytelling. The writing is both funny and tender. Another terrific chapter book series is Captain Underpants with its crazy story of the headmaster who thinks he can save the world. These appeal to a kid's sense of fun, using humour artfully.

Notice how both of these series are rooted in life at school. While picture books tend to explore the world of family and its boundaries, focusing on bedtimes, reading, animals, and the trials and tribulations of being aged 3 to 7, chapter books may take on the world of school and the complications of growing up. While families still feature heavily, so do friendships and the complexities of the child's world outside the family home. This can expand into fantasy (like Kingdom of Wrenly) or have animal characters (like Bad Guys).

Chapter books can be funny, sad, or wise. Best of all is when the author manages to combine all three elements. A beautiful chapter book from a long time ago is *Charlotte's Web* by E.B White. It takes on big themes—life and death—yet makes them accessible and charming for young readers. This lets you think about the possibilities of topics for your own writing. You don't have to shy away from big topics, but do think about how to frame them for young readers.

Graphic Chapter Books

Here's some advice that author Arthur Slade shared with me on how to weave text and illustration for graphic chapter books:

> Chapter books can also be created as a weaving of text and illustration together to make a story. Captain Underpants is a fine example of this: it would not be readable if you took out all the illustrations [this is partly because it switches from a comic-book format and back to prose]. Here the creation of the book becomes slightly more complex. If you are interested in writing this type of book you will have to actually write a script or at least have instructions within your prose for the artist [again the artist will most likely be chosen by the publisher, it is very rare for the author to choose the illustrator].

Now that you know more about chapter books, read a few and try the exercises to see if you want to write one, too.

CHAPTER 4 EXERCISES

Practical Task

Use a title generator on the internet (yes, those exist). When it generates a title you like, write it down. Think about what age group this title would suit. Try to imagine a picture book or chapter book character who could inhabit the world of this title.

Writing: 10 Minutes

Write down the names of five possible characters. They can be the names of real people, or names you mix up from celebrities or book spines (I often use book spines). Take the last name of one and the first of another, mix a few letters, delete, repeat. You never know when one of these characters will wake you up or ask for more time on the page. Polly asked for years with me.

Put your characters into a book for a certain age in your mind. Try them for a different audience. Where do you feel yourself pulled?

Writing: 30 Minutes

Answer each of the following questions either as bullet points or by freewriting:

- What are young children going through now?
- Do you have concerns or worries about what life might be like for a child aged between 4 and 10?
- Has anything struck you in the news recently about children of this age group?
- What makes a 4-year-old laugh? How about a 10-year-old?
- What is *important* for an 8-year-old? Is that different for an older or a younger child?

Taking It Further

PICTURE BOOK

Copy out the text of a picture book you like. Look at how the text works without the illustration. Think about the fourteen double-page spreads (are there fourteen? How many are there? *On the Trapline* has more) and the way the scenes move from one to the other. See if tension and characterization are important. Does the book use rhyme? Make notes on what you observe. How does it impact your own possible book?

Now, write the beginning of a picture book in prose. You pick the topic. Write up to 250 words.

Rewrite the beginning of the same picture book in rhyme, as best you can. This is a challenging exercise, but very useful. Write around 250 words. You may find the rhyming version longer or shorter—the length is less interesting here than how you *shape* the rewrite. Read it aloud to help you with this.

CHAPTER BOOK

Copy out the first 300 words or so of a chapter book. Highlight where there is action. See how the author introduces the character and how they set the scene. Look at the simple sentence structure. Make notes on what you love.

Now, write the opening of a chapter book. You pick the topic. Write three paragraphs.

Rewrite this opening and halve the length. See which words you can remove. Read it aloud to help you with this.

5

The OPTIONS *for* WRITING *for* YOUNG READERS: MIDDLE GRADE *and* YOUNG ADULT BOOKS

FROM MIDDLE GRADE TO YOUNG ADULT

Some of what defines a book for a reader is subjective and purely depends on the maturity level of the reader and complexity of the plot. As always, the more you read, especially books that have been recently published, the more you'll see the differences. For me, writing for middle grade and young adult readers has been some of the most challenging and exciting writing of my life so far. Kids in these age groups are encountering *themselves* in the world, and, I believe, keeping these notions of identity and the bigger world close to the heart of what you're writing is going to help make your book resonate with young readers.

My first published book, *Life on the Refrigerator Door*, wasn't my first foray into writing for younger readers. In fact, the book before, which I called Rosemary Brown and the Defiant Imagination, was aimed at upper middle grade/YA. At least, I thought it was. When I look back, I can see that I wrote Rosemary Brown without knowing much about the age groups I was writing for. I broke conventions unintentionally, and the response from publishers was: *This book is too old for kids and too young for adults.*

That book remains unpublished, lurking on a computer somewhere. *Life on the Refrigerator Door* was the opposite in terms of publishing success. It was published as young adult *and* as adult depending on the country. In some countries, it was published as a dual edition: both as young adult and adult.

I'm hopeful that by sharing with you the conventions for these age groups in this chapter, you'll save yourself my experiences with Rosemary Brown. You can choose to break the rules as a writer, but I want you to do it knowing what you're doing, like I did with *Life on the Refrigerator Door*.

Generally, middle grade is thought of as books for ages 8 to 12, and young adult is for ages 12 and up. This industry standard is what librarians and booksellers often use to determine if a book should be shelved in the middle grade (MG) or young adult (YA) section. While many of the same rules apply to both categories, the differences are really important.

Your young adult reader is technically older, according to the "rules" of types of books for children. While you'll find a lot of blurring with these two categories—an older upper middle grade book might be read by a young adult, and a younger young adult book may be lapped up by middle graders, meaning that sometimes it can be hard to figure out if you're writing MG or YA—but as you read more of these books, you'll begin to see that there are clear distinctions. The more you read, the easier it will be to navigate the words in this paragraph, so that upper middle grade and younger young adult make more sense!

It's worth noting that middle grade and young adult are expanding categories that are getting more layered. Publishers and reviewers will now designate a book as "upper middle grade" (ages 10–14), or "older YA" (ages 14 and up), to acknowledge that some readers are ready for more sophisticated storytelling within their age category. Laura Backes from Children's Book Insider has helpfully broken up the reading list in the back along those lines, to give a sense of what might be considered classic vs. older middle grade, or standard vs. older YA. She's helped a lot with the classifications of these categories.

I'll start with the conventions, then look into books that I love, and hone in on a few extra elements as we end the chapter, helping you think about the genre and the world you might want to create.

MIDDLE GRADE

Generally written for ages 8 to 12, middle grade books vary hugely in length from 25,000 to 50,000 words long, although some can be much shorter or longer. They have more complicated plots than a chapter book, and any illustrations they might have—most aren't illustrated—will illuminate the storyline rather than add new elements. Often, there aren't any illustrations at all. The language may be far more complicated than in a chapter book—readers in this age group (or of these books) are more sophisticated and starting to explore more complicated themes. These readers have a wider vocabulary, but they can also look up unknown words in the dictionary or on their device (something that a reader who is hooked into your novel will happily do). Often, MG novels are written in the third person (he/she rather than I). They look out at the big wide world and introduce lots of characters, just as kids in this age group are starting to look out into the world and explore it.

What I notice is that these books are about kids learning to navigate the world (and this doesn't have to be our world, hence the popularity of portal and otherworld books) as opposed to their emotions (which starts to venture into young adult...). But, saying that, there can and should be emotional development, and readers are fully able to navigate more complicated storytelling techniques—flashbacks, different perspectives, even narrators who don't tell the full truth are all possible. Conventionally, there isn't swearing or sex in books for this age group. Even kissing is often avoided. Crushes and hand holding are where the line often is, again depending on the age of the reader that you're aiming for. In my household, my younger two children (who are 8 and 10) rear back in alarm at the idea of *any kissing at all*. But my twelve-year-old is more curious about that. The type of book that you're writing makes a difference, too. If your book is full of adventure, you might find very little room for any sort of crush. If this category interests you, I suggest reading several

MG books and exploring. Adventure through that portal (do you like what I did there?). In this way, you'll see for yourself the mixture of sophistication, simplicity, and humour that make for great middle grade reading. Do you remember, too, when I mentioned "reading up" and the age of your characters? You'll find that if you want to write about characters who are 13 (-ish) then you're solidly into MG territory.

Again, there are always exceptions to every rule!

YOUNG ADULT

These books are for ages 12 and up. Conventionally, they're 40,000 to 70,000 words long, although some can be much shorter or longer. Even more so than with middle grade novels, young adult readers are seeking sophisticated reads that use more complicated narrative techniques, yet they still want clarity of story overall. If you're starting your novel with the character looking back over something that happened to them when they were a teenager, and they are now an adult, you're moving into adult novel writing. Teens tend to want the experience of the novel to be in the present and now.

They also (like lots of readers) want excitement and shades of grey, and then they want resolution, the ends tied up, the problems solved—or, if you're going to be writing a series, solved enough for this book. That doesn't mean the book needs to be simple. In fact, one book I love (and have mentioned) is *Firekeeper's Daughter* by Angeline Boulley. It uses narrative techniques like flashback and interior monologue, while exploring themes of race, class, family, identity, navigating ancestry, and what punitive justice can do to a community.

My advice is to pick three young adult novels, switch off your phone (maybe you don't have your phone on and beside you all the time like I do!), and get reading. See how fabulous and vivid the worlds are? The books can be deeply real, like anything by E. Lockhart, or they can be utterly fantastical, like the An Ember in the Ashes trilogy by Sabaa Tahir.

The linking thread for me in the YA category has always been that the characters are discovering themselves *as the adults they will become*. The action of the main character—who is always, in the best YA, a teenager—needs to *change them profoundly*. These novels offer young adult readers a way to live different lives, a way to experience a life they may never live, and so enrich the reader's own emotional life. The same as any good adult novel, in fact.

In the young adult novels I've written, I want to immerse the reader in the world of the protagonist so much so that the reader feels themselves under the skin of the main character. I think this is precisely because teens want to experience other lives. They're often so uncomfortable in their own skin that they seek the experience of a novel that takes them into the experience of someone else. *Every Day* by David Levithan, which is about a person who wakes up in the body of a different teenager every day, demonstrates this. This idea so perfectly captures what it feels like to be a teenager. Characters in books that belong in certain genres, like fantasy and sci-fi, might need to be more archetypal—instead of having to struggle with their identity, they are struggling with the world, but it's a much bigger and more complicated world than in middle grade. Tasha Suri, an amazing fantasy novelist in the UK, told me that for YA fantasy often it's the system that needs to change more than the character, who needs to have their own power that they discover in the course of the book. All of these thoughts are for you to play with as you read and think about which type of young adult books you most enjoy.

A lot of adults love to read young adult books. Perhaps they love to relive being that age, or they enjoy the fantastic plots and compelling stories, and the vivid characters and situations that they're in.

NEW ADULT

These books are written with main characters who are aged 18 to 30, often focusing on college or life out in the world just after high school. These books are about young adulthood: when you're an adult but when you haven't yet established family, work, or location. The characters have just begun to walk in adult shoes, and the books are about finding the shoes that fit right. If this is the age category for you, read these books and see how it fits. It's always the way to assess as you read like a writer: does this type of book suit the story ideas I'm starting to have?

TABOO TOPICS—OR NOT?

As you move from MG to YA to new adult, you'll open yourself up to the possibility of writing about darker and darker topics. Middle grade novels can cover dark topics, sure, but you need to keep in mind the age of your readers. Death is something these readers are learning how to process. Graphic sex and gratuitous violence are topics that these readers will probably have difficulty processing. Figuring out what you want your responsibility to be as an author is worth time here.

Young adult and new adult readers are actively seeking topics and themes that offer other lives. Drugs, prostitution, death, loss, terrorism, fear, sex, violence (think *The Hunger Games*), are all topics that young adult writers have explored because their readers are experiencing through the page these ways of being, and these readers are beginning to be mature enough to have tools to process the complexities of our world.

I always ask myself if a scene serves the story or not when I'm writing. If a scene helps tell the story, then most of the time it stays in. Gratuitous sex, violence, etc., just for the sake of trying to lure a reader suggests it's time for a cut. Children and teenagers are clever readers and they will spot attempts by the author to do anything but tell the best story possible. One that helps them navigate their own experience.

CHALLENGES AND OPPORTUNITIES FOR WRITING MIDDLE GRADE AND YOUNG ADULT

Writing for middle grade or young adult readers requires you to think a bit more about the genre, the world, and the structure of your book. These challenges and opportunities are more specific to writing for readers of this age than for younger readers, but you'll find that understanding these will help you flourish with all your writing in the future. Whoever it's for.

Genre

The genre you decide to write in is the type of story you'll be telling, and it's absolutely crucial. Making sure you know the expectation for the type of story you want to write is one of the most helpful ways for you to understand and think about your book.

When you're writing for children and young adults, your audience (the age of your reader) is one key aspect to consider.

But audience, which we've been exploring, is *completely different from the genre* of story (fantasy, sci-fi, romance, thriller, etc.), and *genre expectations* for your age group matter.

Books are bought and sold by their genre—think about how you look for a book when you go to a bookstore. If you love YA fantasy, you head to that section of the store to find a read that fits your expectation. That doesn't mean that you don't want to be surprised as a reader, but it does mean that you expect certain conventions to happen. Learning what is expected within each genre is a useful way for you to think about how you're going to tell your story, especially as you move into writing for older readers. There are many genres for younger readers, but to give you an idea of this let's look at four:

- **Adventure**: Usually the main character heads off on a quest or journey, experiencing personal growth and lots of challenges.

- **Fantasy**: Involving magical elements, it is often set in a fictional universe with mythological influences. Readers want to escape and be drawn into a world where they're immersed. Likely, they expect battles and characters with otherworldly powers.

- **Romance**: The love story is central to the plot and it comes to a satisfying ending. *What If It's Us?* by Becky Albertalli and Adam Silvera is a good example of contemporary YA romance, as is *Eleanor & Park*, a realistic romance by Rainbow Rowell. Subgenres include paranormal and dystopian romance.

- **Science Fiction**: Books like *Across the Universe* by Beth Revis are written based on imagined future scientific, technological, or environmental changes (advances or disasters—disasters lead to dystopian fiction).

A book I love is *Dust* by Arthur Slade. This middle grade novel, set in the Canadian prairies during the Great Depression, is about a boy who has gone missing and his brother who seems to be the only person who cares. It's a fascinating mix of science fiction, historical fiction, and mystery. Just in case you were worried that you had to stick to one genre!

One thing to pay attention to as you read is the genres you tend to love. You'll find yourself drawn to certain books. And when you pick up a book, you'll partly decide if you want to read it because you have certain genre expectations. Before we do that, we'll look at world building for MG and YA, which in certain genres—like fantasy—is so essential. Although it seems like this maybe belongs in the chapter I have for you about scene and setting later on, world building is so key to storytelling for fantasy writers that I wanted to bring it front and centre as you think about the type of book you might want to write. As you read MG and YA, you see how your favourite authors write in certain genres and build worlds in certain ways. As you can't write fantasy without building a world, this is helpful for you while you're prewriting and will help you write the books you most want to write. It's a challenge and an opportunity to explore yourself as a writer and to make your book the best it can be.

WORLD BUILDING

I'm no expert on world building as I haven't ventured into making up worlds in my own writing, so my advice with anything like this is to see how your favourite writers have done it. Looking at the choices they've made can help you discover your own writing path and has always been my first step as I've navigated a writing challenge. Understanding the world your story takes place in is necessary to understand your idea, your characters, and your plot. When you decide to sketch out and then build a world—perhaps for a fantasy or sci-fi novel, perhaps for your own reasons—you have options when it comes to complexity.

Three Possible Ways to Begin World Building

1. **The Most Extreme.** You can make up the entire world, which can put a lot on your plate and require extensive exposition (telling the reader what's going on) but can also give you a lot of freedom to invent and create. You can draw maps, thinking about key things like where the rivers and mountains are and what the climate is like, before you start on the political and social elements of your created place. N.K. Jemisin is my favourite writer for this kind of

work—and her MasterClass online is terrific. She articulates how it can be done in great depth and detail, with wisdom that she's learned from writing some of the most extraordinary books ever.

2. **A Sideways Glance**. Another option for you, if creating a whole world leaves you a bit lost, is to use a contemporary place but change one element. A world just like ours, say, but populated with zombies. Or one where it's normal that people can fly. This gives you a commonality with your reader—they don't have to learn everything about your world as they have shared experiences to connect with (they know what a park is, they know what a school is, they know what a rainy day feels like), and they only have to make the leap into believing there are zombies inhabiting this place. Lots of writers do this—Arthur Slade is a terrific writer to check out for this. *Flickers* is one of his novels where he uses this sideways glance.

3. **Time Shifting/Speculative**. Another option for world building is to move into a different time—either an alternate now where a historical event had gone differently (let's say the pandemic hadn't ended), or in a near alternate future, like in the show *Black Mirror*. It feels contemporary but something is different or parallel about the time, and so the world is new. Perhaps we all have our own robot in a possible future (we do have AI in our computers now…).

Here's a tip that Arthur Slade sent me on one way to get these elements into your book:

> One way is to gradually introduce the fantastical elements into the story. Give the reader details about the real world, and slowly layer in the details about the fantastical elements. This slow process of adding fantastical elements like building blocks allows for the gradual suspension of disbelief. [Mary Shelley's nineteenth-century novel] *Frankenstein* is a perfect example. It begins with a letter home from a ship's captain in the Arctic. It seems like the start of a normal historical novel. Then they pick up a stranger who tells them a horrible tale that eventually turns the story into a fantastical tale.

For each of these different options, the extent of the rules you need will vary. But essentially, what's key is that, as the writer, you balance the need to connect enough for your readers so they understand the new world, but not to pour in so much information that the silvery thread of your narrative is lost. As you're doing the prewriting of your book, thinking, and playing with possibilities, setting up some of these rules will be really helpful for you.

Once you've figured out the possible overall level of your world building, then you can consider and answer the following questions. Your answers will vary depending on how extensive the change is in the world from our own, and yet they'll be helpful.

1. What's the geography of your world like? The landscape? The weather? Where does water come from? Are there physical boundaries?
2. Do you need historical information to understand this world? Have major events occurred that impact it?
3. What's the culture of the people/creatures like? How do they interact? What are their religious/societal/power structures? How are they governed? What do they do for entertainment?
4. What technologies are normal to your world? Has that changed? How is it powered?
5. Is there a system of magic? How does it work?

The more work that you do at this point for yourself, the more you'll have power as the writer of your story to choose which parts you need us to know as readers. The more MG and YA you read, the more you'll see how your favourite writers have included their worlds and made them come alive for you. For now, play with your world. Have fun with it. Make notes. And always keep reading…

WHAT IS STRUCTURE AND HOW DOES IT WORK?

Now that you have an idea of genre and of how to build a world, you might want to think about how you're going to structure your MG or YA book. Remember, at this stage, these are just possibilities and ideas.

The structure of your book is how you shape it on the page, which is, effectively, how the scenes hang together. It's not the plot, it's not the story, and it's not the theme. It's how you get from point A to point B.

Perhaps you use fifty chapters of 1,000 words, say. Maybe you decide to write 10 chapters of 800 words each (which would suit a chapter book, which also requires structuring although hopefully not complicated structure). Perhaps each chapter follows a similar pattern, or you have longer chapters that alternate with shorter ones. Maybe you choose to tell the story in the order that it happened, which is a linear progression: first this happened, then this, then this. Perhaps you have a reason to use a more complicated structure, changing chapter lengths and playing with the order or who is narrating.

For now, just consider options. You can change the structure later, but it helps as you start to write more consistently to have some scaffolding to work with. I shifted the structure of the novel I've been working on at the end of the second draft, because I could suddenly see a better way to do it. But the structure I used before that helped me get to the stage where I saw a new opportunity.

For younger readers, a simple structure is very helpful, as we explored. In the case of a picture book, super simple structure suits the age and developmental stage of the reader. For example, in *On the Trapline*, the story follows a linear path for structure. The complexity of another language layers its beauty. Moshom's memories, which are a huge part of the story, are presented as memories. In *When We Were Alone*, another of David A. Robertson's beautiful picture books, the memories of the grandmother are also presented as memories, but the images allow the reader to experience the flashback. Read it and see how artfully this happens.

As readers get older, structure can and should be more challenging. Not for every book, but certainly as the author you can play with possibilities. Middle grade and young adult readers can handle a more complicated structure, understanding flashback, different narrator points of view, and a more playful or surprising chronology. In *The House with Chicken Legs*, a middle grade novel by Sophie Anderson, there are multiple narrators and the structure is non-linear, moving back and forth through time. The plot is made more complicated by adding in elements of folklore and fairytale.

Perhaps you want to write a 50,000-word YA novel from two perspectives, alternating chapter by chapter, one set in the past and one set in the present, for example. All possible, but make sure you think about how your structure suits your audience and then, more importantly, how it serves your story.

In *Firekeeper's Daughter* by Angeline Boulley, you'll see how the novel introduces the characters in the opening pages. The book hints that something bad is happening, but the main character, 18-year-old Daunis Fontaine, is also dealing with who she is in the world. She feels like she doesn't fit in anywhere. While a lot happens in this book, the structure is linear. And the book stays from Daunis's perspective. That gives readers a strong base to navigate the complexity of the characterization, the plot, which involves an FBI investigation, drugs, and murder, and the themes of race and identity.

CHAPTER 5 EXERCISES

Practical Task

Read the first fifty pages of a MG novel *and* of a YA novel. (Check the suggested reading list if you need guidance as to what to read.)

Ask yourself the following questions:

- Do I identify with the characters?
- Which ones and why?
- What did the author do to connect me to the character?
- Did the story slow down and become boring?
- What was the longest description?
- Which scenes were the most memorable and why?

Writing: 10 Minutes

Cast yourself into who you were between the ages of 13 to 17. What was your life like? What were you most agonized by (for it is an agonizing time)? Did you fall in love for the first time? Suffer heartbreak? Did you fight with your parents? Experience drugs and alcohol—or see friends doing so? Did you suffer your first loss? The exhilaration and drama of teenage life makes for wonderful, glorious writing ground. Make some notes if this appeals to you.

Writing: 30 Minutes

Write for thirty minutes on one of the following:

- At a twelfth birthday party an unexpected guest arrives.
- At an after-grad party someone has died.

- An otherworldly teenager is given a strange gift.
- An 11-year-old finds a portal.

Taking It Further

- Write 500 to 1,000 words of the opening of a middle grade novel. You pick the genre.
- Write 500 to 1,000 words of the opening of a young adult novel. You pick the genre.

PART 2

WRITING

6

FINDING TIME *and* FINDING YOUR FLOW

Fairly regularly, a few days go by when I don't write. My son just walked into the room dressed as a pumpkin, for example, which makes it hard to keep writing but didn't stop me typing. He left the room, the evening trundled on, and I didn't finish what I'd started here. Even on the not-writing days, I'm still in writing mode, though. I make notes, I read, I play with ideas, I focus on craft, I observe something another writer says online.

And I have to be careful, because if too many days go by without writing anything, I start to struggle. What happens to me when I don't write is that I get more agitated with the world. I find everything harder to understand. I'm less patient with my children and my partner. I spend more of my day in a distracted mode, checking my phone, seeking a dopamine hit, and not being in what Mihály Csikszentmihályi, a psychologist, called a state of flow. Jane Yolen, author of more than 350 books, says, "Exercise the writing muscle every day, even if it is only a letter, notes, a title list, a character sketch, a journal entry. Writers are like dancers, like athletes. Without that exercise, the muscles seize up." It's good advice that I strive to follow, even when I don't achieve it.

FLOW

Flow is crucial to what I do as a writer. And I'd love to help you make it central to your practice because as far as I can tell, being in flow is exactly what we need to be our best selves in the world.

In his book *Flow: The Psychology of Optimal Experience*, Csikszentmihályi defined flow as "a state in which people are so involved in an activity that nothing else seems to matter; the experience is so enjoyable that people will continue to do it even at great cost, for the sheer sake of doing it." Each of us have an activity that gets us deep into flow, although some of us haven't been there for a while and so it's hard to remember. These activities are split into four main subgroups:

1. Creative (such as writing, painting, etc.)
2. Cognitive (such as doing a crossword or taking a class)
3. Physical (such as skiing or going for a run)
4. Social (such as sitting with friends and chatting together over a meal)

If you're still not sure quite what flow is, then these eight qualities of it, as described by Csikszentmihályi are helpful:

- Complete concentration on the task;
- Clarity of goals and reward in mind and immediate feedback;
- Transformation of time (speeding up/slowing down);
- Intrinsically rewarding experience;
- Effortlessness and ease;
- Balance between challenge and skills;
- Merging of actions and awareness, losing self-conscious rumination;
- Feeling of control over the task.

For most of us, we have a primary flow activity and a secondary one, and it can be a good idea to choose from two different groups. For me, my primary flow activity is writing, and then I have a secondary one in each of the four groups (skiing, taking a class, enjoying time with friends or family over a meal). You don't need to have as many options, but I'd suggest taking a moment now to write down a flow activity that is primary for you (I'm going to guess writing, but maybe not) and then at least one secondary flow activity.

My advice is to aim to have one flow block of an hour to 90 minutes a day. This thinking, for me, transforms how I get work done. Instead of making time for writing, I'm making time to be in my primary flow activity. I'm making time to feel really good about myself and to be in that effortless space where I lose track of time, where I'm productive and creative and most myself, leaving me filled with essential neurochemicals to deal with the challenges that life throws at me. For me, that looks like writing for at least one flow block a day. Now, as I confessed, it doesn't always happen. But I'm a lot happier when it does. And I'd love that for you. Can you find a window when you can write for 60 to 90 minutes a day? Could that be your flow block? Try it for a few days and see how that type of schedule works for you as a writer.

GOAL SETTING

I'm the sort of person who likes to work with goals. They help me figure out what I want and need to do, and they give me a shape to how I structure my time. And there is evidence that using goals can help you get into flow.

You may find it intimidating to set goals, or perhaps you set goals that aren't in your control, which make getting into flow impossible. Perhaps your goal is to have a number one *New York Times* bestselling children's book. There's nothing wrong with wanting your book to reach a million readers, but it's not a goal that you have control over, not really. You do have control over the steps that would perhaps get you there, though. That could look like this:

- *Goal*: In three months, I will have a draft of a picture book. It will be the tenth draft. I will send it to a freelance editor or work with a writer-in-residence at this stage.
- *Goal*: In five months, I will have a list of agents/publishers to send it to. I will send it out.
- *Goal*: If I haven't had an acceptance letter a year from now, I will review the book editorially and decide if I want to self-publish.

And so on.

Perhaps that sort of timeline gives you the heebie-jeebies. It would have probably put me off writing forever if I'd started with a goal and steps like that—a picture book taking a year?! Having published a couple of picture books, the timeline I've shared with you here now seems too short. From idea to sending to editors, *Violet and Victor Write the Best-Ever Bookworm Book* danced through my head and was finally ready to go out into the world over a period of about eighteen months... It took another two years, at least, to be published.

So, if goals like these seem alarming, or stressful, consider pulling it back a little. What if the goal were to draft a picture book over the next two weeks? Or write 1,000 words of your YA opening by a set date? Or perhaps your goal is to do all the writing exercises in this book and to read five middle grade novels within the next four months?

The reason I set goals is because I have to use the time that I have available for writing, and I'm assuming that's true for most of you, too. Unless you have some magical fairy godparent (purple wings, a shimmery dress, pops out of your closet?) or you have a giant trust fund, your time is not your own. Perhaps you have children or other family members who need your love and attention, perhaps you have commitments or traumas that pull you from the page. All this to say, likely you can't be writing all the time, and so when you do have a writing window, you want to use it well.

When I have a writing window, I know exactly what I want to work on because I have a goal set. Then I break it down into smaller daily chunks. For example, my writing goal today is to draft 500 words of this book. For me, that's a manageable goal (if I stop checking my phone and leave my email alone!). For you, your goals might look different. That's normal. It's important to identify your goals and develop a strategy that works for you.

Goals and dreams are two separate things. Your dreams inform your goals. My dreams align well with the life I live now, but when I was starting out, my dream was to have writing time every day. I dreamed of sharing my writing with someone who understood and valued it, who wanted to talk about it with me. I also wanted to write a great British novel and be on the Granta 40 Under 40 list. Some dreams, like the Granta list, stay in the auditorium of the mind: it will never happen as I'm over 40 now. I had to let that go. But some dreams come true.

For me, they came true because I chunked down bigger goals into daily goals and honoured those.

- Write down your writing dreams.
- Now write down three writing goals. They can be for different books or a timeline for one book.
- How do your goals get you closer to your dreams?
- Now, what one thing can you do tomorrow to be the writer you want to be?

CLARITY OF GOALS

Incorporating my writing life into the hurly burly of my days is exceptionally challenging. Let me share what's helped me achieve my writing goals (you're welcome to borrow this approach or find another that works for you): I structure my time by using a weekly calendar hour or two, and then write down in advance what I intend to so that I know where to start. By reducing friction like this, I have clarity when I begin work. That helps me get into flow.

What this means is that once a week, I sit down and handwrite into a notebook (one I don't lose, oddly) what I'd like to get done in the next week, and then I calendar it all in. I go somewhere beautiful to do this (often the Remai Modern art museum, where I take a chair overlooking the river) and it takes about ninety minutes.

I start with what I call a "cognitive load dump" which is where I write down all the things that are dancing around my head like fireflies. That looks like (for example):

- Pay Peter and Tabitha
- Tidy basement
- Sort out invites for my daughter
- Supper—what to make?
- Pick up meds
- Closet total mess
- Time to rewrite novel
- Workout? Ever happening again?
- Ghost work?
- Reach out to charities on One Small Step to get pages updated
- Plan social content for the week
- Text Kara re: event
- Edits on *Dropped!* due
- Nephew's birthday
- Which class am I behind on?

As you can see, it's messy and all over the place. Next, I group things by type.

My page might look like this (notice a few things are gone from the above list—those are the hyper quick things to do and I get them done before I remake the list):

Writing Life

- Invoice A, B, C
- One chapter of…
- Reach out to Agent re: next ghost project
- Final read-through of *Dropped!*

Family and Homelife

- Plan supper/Buy ground beef
- Party invites
- Clear up massive mess in closet
- Order gift for nephew

Health and Self

- Pick up meds
- Schedule gym

Class

- Next video
- Coursework

One Small Step

- Reach out to charities on One Small Step to get pages updated
- Plan social content for the week

The next thing I do, once my brain has stopped spinning, is look at the week ahead and the available time. I take out any meetings I can and reschedule appointments so that I can have blocks of potential flow time. Then I outline my goals for the upcoming week. Usually I start with pie-in-the-sky ridiculous and then have to bring myself back to reality. My goals for one week might start with "write 5,000 words of non-fiction book, complete short story, review edits on chapter book, schedule socials for the week, read three novels for CTV, and send long-overdue invoices to X, Y, Z."

Once I've compared my goals to my calendar, I can see how I'm setting myself up to fail, so I cut the list down to be more manageable and reword it using the language of flow:

- 90 minutes x 4 times working on non-fiction book
- 90 minutes x 2 times working on short story
- 90 minutes x 2 on admin and invoicing
- Read one book for CTV every night in bed

In an ideal week, I put everything into the calendar in blocks of time, and then I head home, make supper, and hang out with the kids. In an actual week, one child gets sick and Yann adds a few things I've conveniently forgotten. The phone rings and I don't ignore it, interrupting my flow block.

And so on.

My system isn't perfect, but it works for me and my life. Mostly. All this to say, if writing is important to you (or you'd like it to be) then I want you to schedule it in somehow.

CONCENTRATION AND DISTRACTION

As a writer, having a space that I work in helps me to concentrate. I tune out the noise and the haste, and put on headphones that dial me in to the same music that I play every day when I start work. My playlist is what's called a Flow Trigger—it gets me into a space where I'm able to concentrate.

My phone just by its sheer existence is a distraction. I leave it in my car, or put it under my chair or in my purse so I can't see it. I have all my notifications turned off, I set it to Dark Mode, and I have no social media apps downloaded on it. I can only be contacted by my partner and my children's schools. Every other call is set to silent.

It still isn't always enough. The phone is pretty and easy and offers a dopamine jolt. I get restless if I haven't checked that shiny screen for a period of time. I heard on the radio the other day that the average that a person can go without feeling restless about their phone is 5 hours and 11 minutes. That seems long to me.

But when I put my phone away, sit in the same chair, turn on the same music, and open a blank page, usually I can get myself into Flow. And write. This is what helps me reduce distraction so I can concentrate. What would help you?

THE PLACE WHERE YOU WORK

Where do you work? The space where you write is important, I believe. Do you have quiet—do you need it? Do you have beautiful things around you to inspire your writing—do you need them? Do you have novels and books-about-writing cluttered round your desk to inspire you—do you want to?

Cast an eye over the space where you might work and think about what you might need to change to make it more conducive to writing your stories. Maybe you don't have somewhere in your home—can you find a nice café? Or a library? Perhaps a pretty park, but not in a prairie winter! Although even in summer, the mosquitoes and heat might be distracting.

I sit on my sofa with my laptop, although I have a perfectly good office upstairs. The sofa suits me just fine for now. When I start edits on my novel, I'll head over to my co-working space on Broadway. I don't quibble with these funny little quirks. If I need to be on Broadway to work on the book, that's where I'll go.

What is your space like?

What quirks do you have for your own creativity?

PROCESS

The actual writing process requires a certain amount of letting go. Usually, for me, it looks like opening up the computer, putting on my headphones to tune out the noise, and starting to write. For the first few minutes, the writing is awkward and self-conscious. It doesn't flow, it doesn't feel good, and then time starts to slide and I disappear into the actual text, dissolving into the words and sentences, becoming them, almost. I like to have a notebook beside me so I can make notes of anything that's bothering me as I write.

These notes can be writerly, like: NEED MORE ABOUT THIS CHARACTER'S BACKSTORY IN MY HEAD.

To: CALL DENTIST TO REBOOK APPOINTMENT FOR JASPER.

Having these notes on hand means that my brain isn't troubled by the things I can't get to when I'm actually writing. Usually, once I'm set up with my notebook, my coffee, a glass of water, music, and my screen, then I can settle into what I'm working on. And to keep myself going, I set myself a goal (as we looked at). These goals are often word-count based—perhaps I intend to write 500 words. Or if I'm editing, the goal will be to get to the end of a chapter (or manuscript if I'm working on a picture book).

The final thing I have to do is remind myself that I'm doing this because I love it: writing is my gift to me. No one cares if I write another word, except me. It matters to me. And I hope that now you feel confident that it needs to matter to you. Draw a little heart in your notebook, like I do, by your writing time. Write a messy, sloppy, yet uniquely-your-own opening on a blank document. Add another word and another. Begin.

CHAPTER 6 EXERCISES

Practical Task

Schedule a writing window for yourself. That could be three hours every Saturday. Or a daily hour that you commit to and block out completely. It's time to do this now for you—the only way you can be the writer you want to be is to make time for it and honour that time as important. It's time to start writing in a regular way.

Writing: 10 Minutes

Describe what you want to get out of writing. Be honest and wild! This could be:

- I want to be a *New York Times* bestselling author.
- I want to finish a chapter book for my family to enjoy.

Now, it's your turn.

Writing: 30 Minutes

Write down some writing goals for yourself. Try to give these a timeline. That could look like:

- I'll finish a draft of my middle grade novel in 100 days.
- I'll write every day for one hour before my kids/pets/ family get up.

Now use the rest of your thirty minutes to try some calendaring. I schedule in time every week to look over my calendar. For me, it's a necessary first step to avoid procrastination. I finished this book by scheduling time like this. Can you block out time in the next week for writing? Try this and see if it works for you.

Taking It Further

Try my technique of listening to the same songs over and over and see if it works for you. Choose a playlist. I use a ready-made one at the moment. It's the CBC Afterdark Daily playlist on Spotify and it's the right mix of lyrical and non-lyrical. Another playlist I've used is Flow Triggers from Rían

Doris over at the Flow Research Collective. You can choose one of these or make your own by pulling out your favourite songs.

Creating a playlist for a book you're about to write can be a brilliant way to get primed for writing a draft.

7
STORYTELLING

SENSE OF STORY

A sense of story is intrinsic to us as human beings. Philip Pullman says, "After nourishment, shelter, and companionship, stories are the thing we need most in the world." We've told stories since the beginning of our ability to communicate. In this chapter we're going to look at some terminology and ideas around story arcs, plotting, and narrative, but I want you to keep in mind that you probably already have a strong sense within you of what a story is. You *know* when you watch a movie when it doesn't work, and when it does. You *know* when you read a book when it doesn't feel satisfying, and when you want to read it again. Hopefully this chapter helps you articulate these deeply felt notions and, in turn, helps you think about how to make your own storytelling stronger. In this chapter, together, we focus in on the words that writers use to describe the architecture of their books, but a chapter isn't enough for everything there is to learn on this.

At the end of the chapter, I recommend some further reading if you want to dig deeper, and, as always, I give you some writing exercises to try. I also recommend several books for you to read that will deeply enhance your understanding of the underpinnings of story architecture, so that you can save yourself some of the mistakes I've made: these suggestions are at the back of this book. Make notes and enjoy the adventure!

BECOMING A GHOST TRANSFORMED MY GREATEST WRITING WEAKNESS

I've always been the type of writer who loves that feeling of flow I described in the last chapter, and it's hard for me to delay gratification. I get an idea, and before I know it I'm writing reams of words. Sometimes this has worked for me, but most of the time I run out of steam. Or I finish a draft and it makes no sense to any other reader. The manuscript maybe has moments of beauty and grace, but nothing to hold it together. The tone slides and the characters are confusing, they don't have a purpose, because *I* don't have a purpose on the page. The point for me of writing the book was for the pleasure of writing it, to understand my little bit of the world better.

But even though it was never part of the intention, I have an urge to share that bombastic draft with the world.

My genre is unclear.

The structure is messy.

I can't sum up the story in one line. I can't sum it up in ten.

The characters are too much like me. All of them.

Yet I want that external validation of a reader, without having done the work I need to on those key architectural elements: genre, structure, character. To gather 5,000 to 80,000 words and expect them to be cohesive without any planning can be a lot of fun, but it doesn't result in a book.

My writing path has been one where I repeatedly put out work that wasn't ready, getting rejections along the way. This didn't stop when I got published—in fact, it carried on for years. I knew it was a weakness. I knew from rejection letters and abandoned projects that I had to figure this all out. I read craft books before, books with titles that used the word "plot" or "outline," but I never grasped how to implement what they were trying to teach me.

Yann, my partner, is a very good writer. When I say that, I mean that line by line he's able to take a sentence and create beauty. But one of the things he also does—which is completely opposite to how I work—is he uses his time to do research and to structure what he's intending to write *before he begins any writing at all.* This process can take years. For him, writing a book without structure is like building a building without knowing its purpose.

When I've launched myself off into another book, having done a little breezy research and barely any structural thinking, he's been perplexed. My free-and-easy approach had a lot of benefits for me throughout the years (it was a lot of fun and got me into flow super fast), but it had huge cons, as I've just intimated. I've thrown away far more words than I've published, and regularly I've written tens of thousands of words only to abandon the book. Putting aside a project you've loved and yet you've got lost in is miserable. I will come back to this later on.

My writing life was merrily and miserably going along in this vein. Some books worked for readers, others never got the editorial green light. Then I started working as a ghost writer (this means that I write books for other people, of which they are the author). I learned all of a sudden how to structure a book *because I had to.* I couldn't start a book and flow away when I was working as a ghost. I had to prepare a clear outline and proposal for my author. I had to understand the story and line up the chapters and scenes before I wrote anything very much at all.

Now, I've learned to spend more time at the beginning of a project asking myself questions before I leap into a draft because, ultimately, I want to share my books with readers. To do that, I need to respect that the book I'm writing has to hold together in a satisfying way.

PANTSER OR PLANNER

There's a lot of talk in the writing community about whether a person is a "pantser" or a "planner." *Pantser* is a slightly unpleasant word that means someone who flies by the seat of their pants and just writes. A planner is someone who plans. I've learned to put myself somewhere in the middle, where I have a brief plan that I return to, checking in and changing as I write. Because writing with no plan at all only gets me a finished book half the time.

Discovering what sort of writer you are will help you. Knowing that different books need different skill sets when it comes to planning or freefalling into words also helps. Sometimes a book requires that I plan more extensively (for a more complicated structure, for example). And sometimes, I write something just for me that puts me deep into flow—messy, glorious, and all mine. No plan.

Decide if you want to plan your book, pants it, or—that lovely middle ground—sketch a rough plan and write.

USEFUL WORDS AS YOU THINK ABOUT YOUR STORY ARCHITECTURE

There is a lot of information out there about architecture. I want you to be able to keep writing, keep sketching out ideas, and perhaps, if you're a planner, write a plan. Having these words on hand is helpful as you navigate this. Some of these words might be common parlance for you, others might be where you want to dig deeper. Think of this as a mini-glossary for you to turn to and explore.

Central Dramatic Question

The Central Dramatic Question is basically a complicated way to ask: what does your character want?

Call it character motivation, call it a central dramatic question—call it Knuffle Bunny if you like!—but you need to know the answer to this for every book you write (unless it's a high-concept board book). What does your character most desire? How does that change from page to page? In *Knuffle Bunny Free* by Mo Willems, Trixie wants Knuffle Bunny. But, more than that, her deeper desire is to grow up. It's a beautiful dramatic question for a children's book. It gives the story a purpose and the reader something they want to know.

Chronology

The chronology is the order of events as they took place. When it comes to writing a book, you can play with the timeline for effect, or keep the events in the order that they occur. As I looked at earlier, for younger readers a simple chronology is a useful rule. Often, it's a helpful tool for books for any reader, though.

Flashback

A flashback is a scene in a narrative where the character either remembers or is back in time (perhaps this is done by dating the section with the historical date). This reveals something the reader needs to know.

Language: Cadence, Rhyme, and Rhythm

Every line matters in your book. Although this is more obvious in a picture book, it's still true of the longest novel. When you get to the editorial phase, you'll have to hone and rework every word of your book to make it the best it can be. The very best way to hear your work as another might read it is for you to read it aloud. It's a terrific technique to employ in the editorial process. For now, try to choose the best words and know that you'll come back to line editing later in Chapter 11.

Narrative

The narrative is the story of the book—what happens, and then what happens, and then what happens next. The narrative arc is the shape of that—think about beginnings, middles, ends. Each key character will have a narrative arc in a great story. For younger readers, likely, you won't want to have more than one key character.

Outline

An outline is a written document, which can take any number of forms and, like a map, guides you as you write your book. When I outlined *Polly Diamond and the Magic Book*, I used six squares and filled each with what event happened next (I did this after writing 300 drafts—again, not a route I recommend).

The squares look like this:

- Polly, who is about to welcome a new baby brother to her home, receives a magic book.
- She learns everything she writes in it comes true.
- She wants a bigger house, and so writes one.
- The house is out of control. She accidentally turns her sister into a banana.
- Polly tries to fix her mistakes and makes everything worse.
- Polly digs deep and writes a better story (expressing herself—which is the theme!). She is able to squeeze her new brother into her home and heart.

Once I had that outline, I could make choices: do I want to use first or third person? How many chapters do I want? Which scenes do I want? As I've developed as a writer, I now list the scenes and timeline of the story to help myself stay on track. But it took me a long time to do that. The actual writing for me, after all, is so fun!

You can use squares when you outline, or you can write it as a dense block of text (my outlines now look like a short story). Understand at this stage that the outline is a sketch. You can come back to it later once we've looked at character, setting, and scenes in more details. You can delete it, you can play with it, and you can decide you're going to write it, or put it away forever. There are lots of ways to outline; in fact there are entire books written about outlining. I've read several of them. Currently the type of outline that suits me is the one we use at The Novelry, where we use a one-page-plan method. It works for me absolutely!

Remember that your outline doesn't need to be set in stone, and in fact it's preferable if you think of it as a living and breathing document. Shift and change your outline as you write: it's much easier to do that than to rewrite 60,000 words. Trust me, I've done the 60,000-word total-rewrite path for a long time and it's gnarly!

Plot

The plot of your story is the sequence of responses your character has to the events that happen, events *caused by the character*. How the character reacts to these events impacts the story to affect the eventual outcome, which in turn changes the character.

How you structure that sequence of events, which scenes you choose to share, and the way the plot impacts the character and how they rise to the challenges are all the choices you get to make when you begin outlining (or as you pour words onto the page). The thing to keep in mind is that your theme and your plot work together. You want to spend time once you've discovered your theme to think about the best way to explore it on the page (we look at theme in more depth in a bit).

Let's say you want to look at the theme of GOOD WILL ALWAYS WIN. This sets you up to write a story that has certain plot events that might happen. You may want a good side and a bad side, let's say, and you want to see how that plays out in a dramatic fantasy novel. Or perhaps you want to use a classroom as a metaphor—one character in the class is terribly good, and one bad (The School for Good and Evil series comes to mind). As you play with this, it might get you thinking about whether your theme would be more interesting if you slid it over to this: no one is all good or all bad. That might serve your classroom story better, perhaps?

As you play with the ideas of the plot and the theme, you'll see that key to all of this is the character. The way that your character tests your theme is what brings your story energy and throughline. Character is a whole chapter unto itself in the next section as we dig deeper into our work.

When it comes to making all of this happen on the page, it's incredibly challenging for me. Some of you will be plot magicians. Others, like me, will take a whole writing life to be able to achieve that balance of plot, character, theme, genre, and story that makes a book work. And, oh, it will be fun trying to figure it out on the page in first one book and then the next.

Point of View

Stories are told from a point of view. Mainly, this can be first person (I went to the store), second person (you went to the store—rare!), or third person (she went to the store). Third person has different levels. Your book can be told from one character's point of view, or from multiple characters'.

Here are some questions for you to ask yourself: Does the character speak in the first person or would the story suit third person better? Is your story told from the point of view of a narrator or of one of the main characters? Or even multiple characters?

A first-person narrative might sound like this:

> I woke up early and told myself not to bother opening the window. I didn't want to look out there and see the devastation. Not again.

See how intimate and visceral it is? The limitation of this voice, however, is that your character has to be part of every scene. You can try and have them listening at doorways and reading other people's letters, but if there are storytelling elements that the character simply can't be part of then the first person is a tricky one to use. You also need to stay in the character's voice all the way through the text. If you decide to use this point of view, think about the words your character is likely to use and words they can't possibly use. For example, a teenager probably won't sound stiff and formal—unless it suits your theme and story for them to do so.

Here's an example of second person (the you voice):

> You woke and peered through the dirty window. It wasn't any better today so you pulled down the blinds. You were so hungry you ate the last of the crackers last night. Crap. You have to go outside now. You need food.

This voice is rarely found in children's fiction, but that doesn't mean you can't use it. It's daring to try it, and hard to pull off well, but it can be done. I wouldn't recommend it for a picture book, but, saying that, you might have the perfect reason to use it in your next picture book and show me how beautifully it can be done.

Here's an example of third person, limited:

> She opened her eyes and stared at the ceiling. Goddamn it. Another day of this hell. She reached for the blinds but then decided not to bother. What was the point of opening them and looking out there?

This voice gives you a slight distance from the character, but still stays close. I'd recommend if you use it to stay "on the shoulder" of your main character throughout the narrative. As soon as you start to shift point of view, it makes the reading experience choppier. Like this:

> She opened her eyes and stared at the crack in the ceiling.
>
> Martin touched her soft hand. "I think we should talk," he said. His stomach hurt. He had eaten the last of the crackers last night.
>
> Another day of this hell. She pulled away from him and reached for the blinds.
>
> Martin hated her in that moment.

The reader doesn't know who to follow. This technique is actually called Third Person Omniscient because the narrator can "see" everywhere and weirdly floats above the whole story, dropping in and out of people's heads, and it can be a wonderful way to write. But, generally, it's extremely hard for emerging writers to pull off well. I don't use it. I find it too hard to do well. It gets in the way of me telling a good story.

If you decide to use it, I'd suggest staying with one character for one entire scene, as I mention in the section on Voice. A lot of good middle grade writing uses the technique of staying with one character for one scene but then shifting to another character (maybe the bad guy) for the next chapter or scene.

As you read, pay attention to the points of view you enjoy, and the ones that don't work for you. I've noticed a lot of YA is in first person and a lot of middle grade is in third, but you may not find that to be true. I've also noticed when I'm reading with my kids that first person is trickier for them to understand in picture books—they get confused about who "I" is. They like diary formats, though, when first-person voice is used easily and well.

Scenes

A scene is a discreet subdivision of your story, where something happens. An editor once told me to think of scenes as pearls on a necklace, the structure of the book holding the pearls together like the string. We'll look into how to write a scene in Chapter 9.

Theme

Each of us as writers have a theme that we come to over and over again. We don't have to share this with the world—think of it as the hidden deeper resonance of the work: what questions or ideas is the book exploring? There can be more than one theme that speaks to you as a writer, and different readers can come away with different thematic experiences when they read your work. For example, in *Firekeeper's Daughter*, the themes could be the power of community, or good against bad. But really, to me, that book is about the importance of identity for a teenager navigating the world.

The big question that plays in your mind as a reader is the theme. As a writer, think of it as the question you ask yourself as you write. Once you think about it like this, you start to see what your interests and passions are (some of you get points right now because you remember that in the chapter on having ideas, I got you to think about your own interests and passions). Look back over other things you've written. Think about the books you love and what they explore thematically. For me, in the past, my theme has been: *we cannot understand ourselves unless we express ourselves.*

As a novelist and writer of fiction, I wouldn't express that directly. Instead I use story and character to explore whether my belief is right about the world.

Tense

Choosing a tense for your book and sticking with it makes the reading experience easier, especially for young readers. Verb tense shows the time in which the action in the scene takes place. E.g.: She has (present); she had (past). Present tense and past tense are both used in various ways in children's books.

But notice in the following paragraph how tricky it is when a writer shifts tenses:

> Maggie sits in her room, flicking through the paper. She's turning the page when she sees Emily's photo. What was Emily doing in the paper? Maggie jumps up and runs to the kitchen. "Mom," she shouts. "Mom, where are you? Emily's dead." Maggie feels the tears running down her face. She couldn't stop crying.

Look at the same paragraph written entirely in the past tense:

> Maggie sat in her room, flicking through the paper. She turned the page and saw Emily's photo. What was Emily doing in the paper? Maggie jumped up and ran to the kitchen. "Mom," she shouted. "Mom, where are you? Emily's dead." Maggie felt the tears running down her face. She couldn't stop crying.

The past tense creates a little distance, but has a great storytelling feel. Flashbacks and memories can be hard to incorporate in past tense, however. The only way to master this is to practise, practise, practise on the page.

Here's the same paragraph, including a flashback, written in the present tense with the flashback in the past tense.

> Maggie sits in her room, flicking through the paper. She turns the page and sees Emily's photo. Emily who she met the first day of school. Her best friend. She remembers the argument they had yesterday. The terrible things she said.
>
> Maggie jumps up and runs to the kitchen. "Mom," she shouts. "Mom, where are you? Emily's dead." Tears run down Maggie's face. She can't stop crying.

The present tense gives an immediacy and an easy way to use flashback and memory (by shifting to the past tense). But it can feel a little breathy and rushed. You make the choice as to which you prefer in your own writing.

Voice

One question you'll need to ask yourself is, *Who is telling this story?* This is the question of *narrative voice*. Is the voice funny or melancholic? Does it use long words or short? Is it chatty or formal? What suits your story, or your *theme*, best?

Hopefully by asking these questions I can help guide you, but remember that *you're* the only one who knows the answers. And those answers will be different for every book you write, so you'll have to ask yourself these questions again. And again.

One answer I can suggest is this: I would argue that the best way to tell your story would most likely be to stay in one voice per scene. Shifting voices mid-scene is tough on a reader and makes for choppy reading. As you move through the age categories, there are reasons to write from more than one character's perspective, but you'll have noticed in your reading that when authors do this, often they start a new chapter, and they definitely don't shift mid-scene. They also don't tend to do this for younger readers as it can be confusing for little kids. I can hear my younger sons trying to figure out who is telling the story when an author complicates this unnecessarily.

CHAPTER 7 EXERCISES

Practical Task

Write down five things that could be your theme. Remember, no one ever sees this, and you can't get it wrong. You can edit it anytime, but have a possibility at the back of your mind underpinning everything you work on. Here are some starting points to get your excited:

- No one is all good or all bad.
- Secrets will always come out.
- Families are the creators and solvers of problems.
- Good will win.
- When we are our most authentic, we succeed.

Writing: 10 Minutes

Take one of the themes above and free-write for ten minutes. I hope through trying the freewriting exercises up until now that you've started to see how much you can write in ten minutes!

Writing: 30 Minutes

Write an outline for your book. I like to use a single page to describe what happens and then what happens next. You can use bullet points. You can use a visual. For young readers, the outline may end up being longer than the final text, but that doesn't mean this isn't going to be a useful tool for your story.

Taking It Further

Pick one of the books on storytelling that I've listed at the back of this book. Curl up with it every day and deepen your understanding of this vast area.

8
CHARACTER

WHERE DO CHARACTERS COME FROM?

As I get ideas for a story, characters float into my mind, just as happens for Alice Walker, who writes, "If you're silent for a long time, people just arrive in your mind." Some years ago, a teenager who wrote an online advice column popped into my head, and I realized I wanted to write a story about a girl who was determined to control her life (which became my YA novel *40 Things I Want to Tell You*). In the story, she was confident advising other people how to live, but she had to understand she can't control the world and that we all make mistakes. So, there she was in my mind. This teenage advice columnist. But who was she? How could I know the things she was going to do in the book until I'd got to know her?

I started with her name: Amy Finch, nicknamed Bird. Having a name makes writing easier for me. From her, the story began to unfold, as Anne Lamott describes, "Plot grows out of character. If you focus on who the people in your story are, something is bound to happen."

In this chapter, we'll begin by looking at your main character. It's important for us as writers to know how our protagonist might act and react, as we'll look at shortly. Together, we'll think about the layers that make your main character who they are: their characteristics, physical attributes, history, and flaws. And then we'll look at the rest of your story's cast before getting into the exercises at the end. If you find that your book is stuck, try strengthening your character work to make your main character and cast come alive.

ACT AND REACT

In the opening of your book, it's important for the reader to see the character in their normal life in the way that they've always been. And then, in the best stories, something happens that challenges their way of life and their future. I believe to tell a good story you have to have a character act and react, which makes your story change and move forward. It took me years and years to understand this concept.

Look at these two examples:

> A teenager is sitting in a room looking out the window, thinking about his lost love, re-reading a letter.

> A teenager with agoraphobia gets a letter from his lost love. Tentatively, he digs out his suitcase and starts packing.

Which story is the one you'd want to read? In the first instance, the teenager isn't *doing* anything. I'd pick the second story every time.

If you make your characters act and react your story will be propelled forward as if the character is the one pumping the story's blood through its body.

When a character acts and reacts, it changes the events of the story. In the second example, because the teenager starts packing—*acts*—the story has a place to go. The plot is impacted, the narrative moves forward. How your character makes the story change because of how they act is what a reader wants to know. And this is true for readers of all ages.

As the character *acts* and causes things to happen, they need to *react* to whatever they've put in motion. The word *react* means two things: responding emotionally and responding by taking action. I believe that your job as a writer is to show me as your reader how your character reacts to the events of your book; for example, how the little girl *reacts* to the frustration of her most magnificent thing *not* being what she wants, in *The Most Magnificent Thing* by Ashley Spires.

CHARACTER FLAWS AND LAYERS

As we've looked at, the way your character behaves makes them who they are, and makes the story what it is. What's crucial to think about now is what weaknesses or flaws your character has to overcome. This is because as your character starts to overcome their weaknesses, wrestling with them, they change their life, *which is what your story is about*. A line from Rainbow Rowell helps me focus my main character:

"You look like a protagonist." This, in turn, helps me sharpen my whole story.

You might be working on a picture book and thinking, hmmm, this isn't what I need to work on. But actually the journey of your main character is key to storytelling. In *The Most Magnificent Thing*, for example, our protagonist is very easily frustrated. She has to overcome her own temperament in order to make that magnificent thing, and that makes the story. The main character is vivid and true and real *because* she's imperfect and has to overcome that challenge. Her nature creates more problems for herself, and then those problems challenge her to change. And that makes the story.

Thinking about your story, your theme, and your character together is a process.

It might look like this: Perhaps you want to explore how *right and wrong are a spectrum*. Let's say you love reading middle grade. And you want to write a dystopia. Maybe you're really interested in climate change.

Perhaps you put your character on a boat with ten other people and they have to survive in this new watery world.

Knowing all of those things, *who* would be a great person to put into this story?

1. An older man who has left his wife for a younger woman.
2. A 12-year-old who has a dark secret, a ton of survival skills, and who is sure they are always right.
3. A perfectionist tween who was expelled from school before the waters rose.

4. A teenager who is unable to manage their homesickness, but who wants to find their mother.

Because I've already decided I love middle grade novels, numbers one and four are out. Those characters are too old to be interesting for a middle grade reader. For today, number two is the character I want to get to know better. That doesn't mean this is the character I'm going to have as my main character for sure. I don't know that yet. I don't have to decide. Instead, I get to play. One way for me to do that is for me to get to know my character better.

Getting to know your character helps you think about how your story is going to change and grow. Who does that character see in the mirror? What's their story and why? And how does this impact your plot? This rule of thumb has always worked for me: if you find that your book is stuck, try strengthening your character work and make the story come alive.

CHARACTER DESIRES AND HOW TO USE THE INTERVIEW

You've probably heard this before, but it's worth reflecting on as you create your main character: having a character who wants something is much easier to write about. That's because all of us want something, and when we read about someone who has a desire, we understand their motivation. Glancing back at the possible characters I suggested above, the teenager who is homesick but who has to find their mother has an interesting story already starting to shape. The teenager's desire (to find their mother) goes against their personality. And so, we're beginning to make life easier for ourselves as a writer because the story is shimmering just in front of us now.

As your possible story unfolds like this, I recommend that you interview your character as if they are a real person. Sit them down (imaginatively) and ask them about their life. Where do they go to school? What does an ordinary day look like? What do they most want in this moment? What do they wish they'd never done? At the end of this chapter, I have a list of questions for you to try so that you know the person you're writing about. In the book that I'm working on, I realized halfway through the first draft that my main character wasn't very interesting. I share this with you because I want you to know that it's okay to have some ideas about your character, to answer all the questions, to be writing *and then to change elements* as you learn more about your book.

I always ask myself: Why this person? Why this story? Why now in their lives? Remember how with Polly Diamond it wasn't until she was a bit older that I finally knew how to write her book? Be open to the places the story itself can take you, as your character begins to lead.

CHARACTERISTICS, HABITS, BODY LANGUAGE, AND SPEECH

All characters have sayings, gestures, habits, and personal objects that are unique to them, things that are typical of them as a person, the traits that make them unique. One way for you to get to know who your character might be is to think about the objects they value.

If a 13-year-old girl lives in an apartment with nothing but fluffy teddy bears and Hello Kitty dolls lining the walls, that shows you something about her, right? If she has a small dog that she dresses in sunglasses, if she only drinks cream soda with ice made from the water of a river in Fiji, if she has a romance novel in her purse, do you get a sense of who she might be? The things a character owns are hints for a reader.

Now, imagine you have two suitcases to go through. One is full of neatly folded clothes, a blank diary, and a photograph of an older woman, looking sad. The other bag is messy, stuffed with scrunched up T-shirts and random clothes, and a novel by Kenneth Oppel pokes out. What guesses would you make about the owners of each of the bags?

What do your characters want to buy, and what does it say about them?

What books does your character own and read? What movies?

Every object that you place in a character's possession gives you as the author the opportunity to give the reader hints.

Moving on from objects, think about how your character speaks. Is there a particular word they use all the time, a quirk of language (each character in your book might have one of these, which is a great way for a reader to feel like they are getting to know your characters)? I'm not suggesting you force a dialect here. Instead, think about words your person always uses. Perhaps they say "absolute magic" often. Or does your character enjoy long words that most people never say?

Now think about the way your character talks. Do they shout? Or whisper? Do they rattle out sentences or think before they speak? The more you know, the more you can hint at in your book. All these details make a character different from someone else on the page, and make them real to a reader.

Does your character have a characteristic gesture? Do they wipe their nose all the time or pick at their front tooth? Do they giggle a lot? And what are their habits? What does your character do every day, every week?

As a writer, knowing these details gives me clues as to who the person is that I'm going to be hanging out with for the next little while of my life. Sometimes, I discover the character as I write a draft. But often, I do a lot of work at the beginning of my book, getting to know the character so that I *can* write.

DIVERSITY IN YOUR CHARACTERS

We've looked at this question when it comes to story and who has the right to tell a story. It's worth pausing again to think about your main character and your cast of characters.

When a writer adds in a diverse character to give the illusion that they are being diverse, reverting to stereotypes, this is called tokenism. Many novels make the mistake of adding in a character of colour or a neurodiverse character or a character with an underrepresented sexual orientation as a best friend or back-up character, for example. Triple check that you're not writing a character because you're marking off some awful check box.

It's really important you think about each of your characters, what they add, what you need to tell your story best, what your knowledge of your character is, what your gaps are, where you are stereotyping and how, and where you are stepping into a space that you need to research. And yes, you also want to make sure that your cast isn't all alike. I want to direct you at this point to the workshops at www.writingtheother.com to help you make the best choices for your book, yourself, and your readers.

If you have included a character or characters who come from a different background or heritage as one example, you could consider paying a sensitivity reader. I value the input that sensitivity readers have given me for my work, and recommend you look into this. If you'd like to learn more about sensitivity readers and how the process works, there are some great online resources.

PHYSICAL ATTRIBUTES

So, we've thought about our characters' habits and gestures, and once we've done the character interview in the exercises at the end, you'll even know their favourite foods. We've got to know them on the inside. But what do our characters look like and how can we write this? Stephen King gives a good example in his masterful book *On Writing*. He says if you describe a character as a "pimply faced high school outcast" you should trust that we've all met someone like that. He suggests letting the reader fill in the rest using their imagination: "Description begins in the writer's imagination, but should finish in the reader's."

Before you even think about how much a reader needs to know, you need to know for yourself what your character looks like. I use random face generators until the person in my mind matches the person generated. It helps me to have a sense of what the person looks like. Perhaps you have an image in your mind that you can sketch.

Tips for Writing Physical Description

1. The best time to include physical description is when you introduce your character. If you don't tell your reader until the tenth chapter that your character has a limp or woolly grey hair, they'll be surprised (and annoyed) you didn't give these details before. They will have an image of the character in their heads from the first moment they meet the character on the page. You can and should tell crucial physical details fast.

2. You want to avoid a character looking in a mirror (which has been done a lot, especially in YA fiction), and think instead about how the physical aspects of your character change how they interact with the scene they are in. Do they have to dip their head to go through a doorway because they are so tall?

3. Pay attention to how your favourite writers do this in the books for the age groups you love. It's different between a book for younger readers (where you need barely any physical description as the book will have illustrations) and a middle grade novel, where readers like to know what their characters look like.

OTHER KEY CHARACTERS

Now it's time to think about all the other people in your book. I'd recommend that you get to know each of the key players in your cast. If we're going back to the boat story, the one with the 12-year-old who has survival skills, I'd think about who else was on the boat. The other important characters would get the same treatment my main character had: interview, physical attributes, favourite things, etc.

Take time with each of your characters, interviewing them and getting to know them, so that you feel confident that you have companions for your trip. Choose people who are *interesting*, if not likeable (not everyone can be likeable or you'd be bored, right?).

And keep in mind that all this work *is for you*. You don't have to stuff it all into the novel as if you're feeding a foie gras goose. In fact, most of this work is going to stay off the page, enriching your book because you know your cast well so you can see how they *act* and *react* because of who they are.

Bit-Part Characters

Your bit-part characters are the ones who appear to add texture to your book. They don't last long and have no impact on the story. You get to play here, texturing in fun details of people you want to populate your book with. Maybe the barista has an eyebrow piercing. Or the person on the bus has a kitten in their jacket pocket. Or the kid in class wears a locket with a very old photo in it... These tiny details give the reader enough to visualize the character as much as they need to, and then they can move on to the magic of your story.

Tips for Writing Your Cast

1. Add to the questions (birthdays and star signs might interest you, siblings, perhaps pets?).

2. Notice as you go through if one of your characters can be merged with another. And think about how each of your characters serves your story.

3. Notice if several of your characters have the same first letter for their name. It actually makes for tricky reading. Changing this is an easy way to help distinguish your characters from each other.

CHAPTER 8 EXERCISES

Practical Task

Think about this quotation by Ernest Hemingway: "When writing a novel a writer should create living people; people not characters. A character is a caricature." Make some notes on what this makes you reflect upon. How is your character a living person?

Writing: 10 Minutes

As a quick way to get to know your character, focus on the things your character owns and their habits. Write quickly and sketch out your person on the page.

- What would your character pack on a trip?

- What objects are in your character's room?
- What books has your character read in the last year?
- What does an ordinary Monday look like?
- What about a Saturday morning?
- What habits does your character have—do they floss?

Writing: 30 Minutes

If you have a character you're working with already, then use that character. Otherwise, just start answering the questions to discover your character on the page. Remember, these questions are for an imaginary character to answer (unless you as the writer decide otherwise). And if your character is a picture book star, then some of these questions won't be helpful. Use your judgment to see what you need to know:

- What's your name?
- Describe where you live.
- What's your earliest memory?
- What's the worst thing you've ever done?
- Who do you love?
- What's your favourite food?
- Describe a perfect day.
- What do you do when you wake?
- In this moment, what do you most want?
- If you could go anywhere, where would you go?

And one bonus question: What did you do the last time you were in trouble?

Taking It Further

Lizzy Goudsmit Kay, editorial director of The Novelry, says: "Challenge yourself to get to know your characters better. If a waitress spilled hot coffee on them, how would they respond? If their car broke down, who would they call? Make sure you know how they behave in everyday situations, and then stick them somewhere unexpected."

How does what you've learned about your character change the storyline? What else do you need to know now that you've read Lizzy Goudsmit Kay's advice? Reflect on your story so far and see if you want to make any changes before you move on.

Think about the layers of this person. Remember, your character will have guilt, shame, stresses, coping strategies, quirks, and a way of being in the world. For books for younger readers, some of this won't be helpful, so keep that in mind!

Answer these questions for your character:

- How does your character present to the world?
- What does your character secretly fear?
- Who is your character's shadow self? Who do they not let people see?
- What do you know about your character that they don't yet know about themselves?
- What is your character's flaw?

9

SCENES *and* SETTINGS

Think of the world of your novel as a stage. As we have our cast now, the events that happen upon that stage are where that cast will act and react. Each of those events occurs within a scene and each of those scenes needs a setting. The writer of a play doesn't expect to get every scene right in the first draft, instead they think about how to pace the story and how to work with a director and scene-setting to add energy, dynamism, and emotional range. *Move this way. No, let's try that over here. Scrap that! Let's try setting the next scene in the playground…*

In the book I've been writing, many of my first draft scenes had the main character walking the dog. Hmmm. I love walking my dog. But that's not a reason to have my character doing that all the time! In the next draft, I'll try her in various settings to shift and change the dynamics of each scene and the overall feel of the book. Think of it this way: your overall novel world is your novel's stage and your reader gets to see the curtain rise on different scenes. The settings of your scenes are a crucial backdrop you get to control. As Nicola Yoon aptly says in her YA novel *Everything, Everything*, "Just because you can't experience everything doesn't mean you shouldn't experience anything." As the writer, you get to choose which setting elements of your novel's world you share with your reader, scene by scene.

SCENES

As I mentioned earlier, one of my editors told me once to think about scenes like pearls on a necklace. Your book will have a series of these pearls, joined together with string (transitions, or scene breaks).

Each pearl will have its own beginning, middle, and end. And each needs to have a purpose for being in your story. It's absolutely normal to write a scene and then decide later that it doesn't really serve any storytelling purpose, so don't worry about this too much for now. You can edit out scenes later. For now, each scene needs to have a reason for being: think about how to increase the conflict as one way to assess the importance of the scene.

Instead of thinking about the importance of each scene overall, for the rest of this chapter, we're going to look at some craft techniques to help you make each scene stronger. Firstly, each scene will have its own setting. If we go back to the stage of your book, this is your opportunity to set your scene in the park, or the schoolyard, or in a desert filled with strange creatures.

Once I have a possible purpose and setting for the scene, I think about the beginning, middle, and end of scenes as having four possible elements *within them*. You can work on these elements to strengthen your writing. From picture book to YA, scenes need some of these elements. What's fun as a writer is deciding which you know how to do well, and which you can work on more.

The Four Elements of a Scene

1. Description
2. Action
3. Dialogue
4. Interior Monologue

By thinking about each of these, we can figure out where we want to dig deeper and where we want to pull back. Some scenes you'll read in the books you love have all the elements, and some have just one or two. Each has a different effect and impact on the reader. Learning how to write each of these elements helps you as a writer in a different way.

DESCRIPTION

Description is used in two ways for scenes. Firstly, description *sets* the scene for a reader: they want to know where they are. In *Dust*, by Arthur Slade, the first scene is three miles from the family farm. Arthur gives a gorgeous weather detail, immediately helping the reader feel the heat and the setting of this scene:

The sun had shifted nearer to the earth in the last half hour or so, so near that the air crackled with heat.

Setting your scene helps your reader to feel fully immersed in the story, and helps them not to feel lost. As you read, notice how your favourite authors bring you into scenes with at least one element of description. Some writers love to layer in reams of description, but if you're writing for young readers, you don't want to get too bogged down. It slows the text for them and makes them feel less accomplished as readers. Getting the balance between sharing the rich setting you've created in your mind and keeping the story going is an art.

Years ago I was sitting in a shaded garden, chatting with the writer David Carpenter. He asked me how I'd written a book with no setting (he was referring to *Life on the Refrigerator Door*, which is a novel written entirely in notes and which has almost no setting reference other than the door of the fridge—only mentioned in the title). I made sounds about how setting didn't really interest me and how it wasn't really important, what was important was character. To me.

I wasn't lying. But it wasn't an honest answer in the sense that there was a second, secret reason. The other reason was that I find description hard—I'm not sure I could have articulated it at the time. Likely, I hadn't confessed it even to myself.

All of us as writers have natural strengths and weaknesses, and one of my weaknesses was setting. I've learned some techniques that make it easier for me to write better settings than I used to, to the extent that now sometimes the setting is the first thing that comes to mind as I begin to play with an idea for a story.

The art of description *isn't* writing every single thing that comes into your head when you imagine a place. Conversely, it isn't what I used to do, which was avoid it totally and hope my reader could locate themselves on the white page. (It worked for *Life on the Refrigerator Door*, but I don't think I could get away with it again.)

Currently, I'm setting the book I'm working on in a prairie town as winter arrives. Perfect, as it's winter now in Saskatchewan and I've got material right in front of my eyes (if I put on a thick coat, gloves, toque, scarf, and ski pants and brave it!).

Some of you will be setting your story in a place you know well, in which case you can make notes directly on what you see and experience as you inhabit or remember that space. Your unique observations are wonderful material as you write—the only trick here is to make sure that you're only using a little of the wealth of possible options for your setting. As Stephen King said about character, your reader likely has a good understanding of the world. They know cold, they can conceptualize a lake, so what detail do you need to add to make it spring to life in their mind? Perhaps a kid's purple glove stuck on a fence post in a snowy street. Or steam coming from a dog's pee. See? I don't need to go on about the cold when I have these elements bringing the story into your mind.

If you don't inhabit the place, but it's a real place that currently exists, then you have options. You can either determine it essential to visit that place (travel and write! The dream!) or you can do research, asking people who live there, googling it, reading about it. If you're writing about the past, then you have to rely upon the reports from people who lived in that time.

And then the other option for setting is for you to invent somewhere, building your own world, which we looked at in Chapter 5.

Writing Description

These questions help me improve my descriptions:

1. Have I got any person in the setting? Having a character in a setting makes the setting come to life. So how do they interact with the place? Which verbs am I using to get the description across? How does my setting reveal character and vice versa?

2. Am I using directions in a clear way? Or have I put the elements in a choppy way for a reader? Just to help you see what I mean here, this description has no visual order to it:

   > The big house at the end of the path was hard to see. Amber walked toward it, lit by a blue orb. It led the way. The snow on the ground crunched under her boots.

   This second version has an order to the direction the character is travelling. We see what she does, following along as readers:

   > The snowy pathway led into the shadows. Glowing blue, the orb bobbed impatiently, illuminating Amber's face. She scrunched her nose against the

> cold as she forced herself to follow the orb, the dark house closer now.

One version isn't right or wrong, but the second is easier for a reader to visualize.

3. Am I using several or all of the senses? Do I need to? Which single element would be the most noticeable?

4. Have I overloaded the description with adjectives and adverbs?

5. Is the description accurate to what I want? Does it satisfy me?

The second way description is used in scenes is how it's used technically throughout: you're not just using the tool of description to set the scene, but to enrich it. Often, we use the first words that come to mind rather than taking the time to actually experience or imagine a richer, more textured description. In your first draft, allow these first words to take up space. But I suggest you make notes when you're not on the page that you can use to enliven, enrich, and deepen the texture of your book: what do you notice when you pay attention to the world that could enhance your story with stronger description?

ACTION

Something has to happen in a scene for it to resonate with a reader, especially a young reader. As you progress through the age groups to the older end, you have more space for interiority and reflection. But that doesn't mean that you want to skip on using your scenes as opportunities for action.

Action happens when your character is required to do something, and it's even better if they want something first. That makes them want to *do* something, which we looked at in our section on character. When a character does something, it makes us root for them. When you put something in their way—something that creates friction, increasing the drama and conflict around the action—your reader turns the pages.

If you distill your favourite movie or book into the five or six key scenes your mind conjures, you'll quickly see how important action is to a story. The moments when things happen are what our mind connects to. We *become* the characters as they do things; as they act and react, we think about what we might do in that moment. Young readers want to experience your story this way, too.

As you think about action in your scenes, you'll start to realize that it happens around the verbs you use. It's good to think about this as you read through stories by your favourite authors. Notice how they introduce action and the effect it has on a reader. Which verbs do they use?

Young readers in a chapter book, say, don't need a lot of breathing room. They enjoy the go, go, go. When you read the Bad Guys series, you'll grasp how much action young readers can handle. Lots! But don't skimp on the other scenic elements just because your character is in action mode. A brush of description, a moment of reflection, a line or two of dialogue can go a long way as your characters race through high stakes. You need a good mix of pacing in your writing. Too much action makes it difficult for a reader to take a breath. Notice when you're reading when you think the author used too much action and forgot the other scenic elements.

Writing Action

1. Use strong verbs. These are the muscles of your writing, and they don't have to be complicated words for kids to be able to visualize the action. Instead of *walk*, try *amble*, *stroll*, *saunter*, *stride*, *trudge*, or *plod*, for example. Keep in mind the age of your reader as you play with this. If I were writing a chapter book, I might use *stroll* or *plod* of these choices, because they are easier to read. If I were writing YA, I might use *trudge* to give clues about the feelings of my teenager.

2. Notice if you've been writing without a lot happening. It's not unusual as a writer to have a character sitting down because *we're sitting down doing the writing*. This is a mistake I've made a lot. Nearly all my characters love to write, and I've had to pay attention to how much sitting around they do. Get them up, get them doing something. Maybe not walking the dog, though. Or not all the time, at least!

3. Raise the stakes. Can you make it more challenging? More exciting? What could happen next to up the conflict and drama? What could your character cause to happen?

4. Just as we looked at with description, think about the order of your sentences. In a fight scene, say, where limbs are all over the place, a little careful arranging of the order of events can make a big difference to what a reader is able to imagine. Read lots of fight scenes to help you navigate this.

DIALOGUE

Good dialogue moves the story forward, conveys believable characters, and feels full of life. It gifts sound and music to your writing because your reader hears your characters' voices. If you're anything like me, words and phrases you keep going back to as an author can make your characters sound very similar to each other (or to *yourself*). But our job as writers is to make our characters sound like *themselves*. That starts as we get to know our characters, and then continues as we look for words and ways of speaking that suit each of them. We went through this as we looked at our characters, and now as we try them out in possible scenes, we can see how those ways of speaking start to sound. Once you have a sense of who each of your characters is (I find the character interviews help here, and sometimes I do the character interview a second or third time once I've been writing for a while), then the dialogue in your scenes will bring pace to help your characters come to life.

Writing good dialogue takes practice and patience. Here are lots of tips for you to improve how you write your dialogue so your conversations crackle on the page.

Writing Dialogue

1. Read dialogue aloud. It's meant to be heard, after all. This will help you to listen to the voices of your characters, noticing the flow and movement of their words.

2. Don't use dialogue to convey large chunks of information (exposition). People don't sound like this: "Since we arrived here at four, to watch for Peter Gambit, the murderer, I've felt hungry." You can see how awkwardly that reads.

3. Dialogue should sound real, but that doesn't mean dialogue on the page is exactly like snippets of dialogue you overhear. When you cut out all the *Hellos*, *Goodbyes*, and boring small talk of daily life, the dialogue reads more fluidly.

4. The best place to hear and learn dialogue is by attending (or reading) plays, streaming shows, or paying attention to conversations around you.

   If you want your character to say, "I need you," think about the words they would actually use. Perhaps they'd say, "I can't—Do you have to catch the early bus?" These slips and hesitations, lies, unfinished sentences, missteps, and unspoken longings are what give your characters depth and resonance. In real life, we don't always say what's on our minds. Notice when you bite your own tongue, and think too about the things you wish you could say to those you love. Thinking about what's not said in the scene can be really impactful for a reader. As readers get older, they can navigate subtext better and better. You might need to spell out more clearly what a character is actually saying for younger readers but be able to pull back for older ones.

5. The nitty-gritty of writing dialogue comes down to punctuation: effective use of quotation marks, periods, commas, and question marks, along with knowing where to put speech tags like "he said." Please don't think this is boring, as it really doesn't have to be. Instead, it's an essential tool for you as a writer. If you were an athlete, you'd be expected to do sit ups; if you were a chef, you'd have to chop onions. As a writer, grammar is an essential tool, making it easier for you to write the dialogue you want. It'll help your work look professional when publishers read it. More importantly, learning how to punctuate speech will help you tell the stories you want to tell.

6. Most readers glide over *he said/she said* as if those words were punctuation. Using too many other tags, like *exclaimed*, *gasped*, *screeched*, *postulated*, *reasoned*, *argued*, *pondered*, *mouthed*, etc., overwhelm the dialogue. Look at:

   "I don't know how to get down!" she screeched. She clung to the branch.

Compared to:

> "Help! I'm stuck." She clung to the branch.

In the second version, the words of the dialogue do the work, not the tag.

7. Think about how your dialogue serves your scenes. If everyone is agreeing with each other, your scene will feel flat. Dialogue gives you an opportunity for conflict and drama.

8. Perhaps one character likes to use a certain word or short phrase, so make sure the other characters don't use that same word or phrase. It's a small distinction, but useful. The best way to make everyone sound different from each other is to actively look out for and notice when your characters sound too similar. Notice words that are unusual that one character might use. Notice if one character speaks more formally and if another is more relaxed.

INTERIOR MONOLOGUE

Interior monologue, which is also called inner dialogue, directly shows a character's feelings, thoughts, and what they see about the world. Some writers like to italicize this, but often it's written as a stream of consciousness or is labelled as thoughts. Notice how your favourite writers share what's going on inside the minds of their characters to see how *you* like to read this.

While that inner voice that we all hear is an essential element on the page in writing scenes in books for adults, revealing character and motivation, it's not the most useful scenic element when writing for younger kids. For the picture book lovers amongst you, you'll quickly realize that for books that are often read aloud, too much interiority is deeply confusing. When my kids were younger, they thought it was *me* sharing my inner thoughts as I read aloud, instead of the character.

Most likely, this technique is one to lean into more as you move into age groups at the upper end of chapter books and beyond. In *The One and Only Ivan* by Katherine Applegate, Ivan's thoughts and feelings are shared, as a perspective on living in captivity in a shopping mall.

In *The Thing About Jellyfish*, a middle grade novel by Ali Benjamin, interior monologue is used to help illuminate the main character's feelings as she makes sense of the loss of her best friend by drowning. Another middle grade novel that uses interior monologue is *The Girl Who Drank the Moon* by Kelly Barnhill. This fantasy novel uses sophisticated interior monologue techniques to show how several characters, including the main character and the witches, think and feel. As you move into YA territory, you'll see interior monologue used more and more heavily.

Writing Interior Monologue

1. Don't use it too often. Less is more with this technique, especially for younger readers.

2. Use it to add something the reader can't know otherwise. If it's clear the character is upset because they're sobbing, you don't need to add *I'm so sad.*

3. Make sure the way your character sounds inside their head is consistent with who we think they are. Keep it consistent with their actions and dialogue.

4. It's always tricky to make it clear who is thinking/feeling when you write interior monologue. Look at the authors you love and how they approach this for the techniques you want to try. I dislike italics, for example, and prefer to drop the thoughts and feelings into the scene as is.

CHAPTER 9 EXERCISES

Practical Task

Spend some time every day for the next week actively paying attention to the places you go. What small and significant details could you note for each place that would help someone else see it? Notice the weather and the sounds you hear. Make notes on how the place feels, on what you notice about other people in the place, and on any plant or animal life in the vicinity. Outside the window of this third-floor lounge, I see two pigeons freewheeling in the bright sky. What do you notice now that you're in observational mode? Could you get into the habit of making notes on place and setting frequently? How would that enrich your writing?

Writing: 10 Minutes

Three characters, one with a secret that one of the others has discovered, are in a schoolyard. Write for ten minutes some of the conversation that follows. Make each character sound distinct, think about what is not said, and add in elements that show us where the scene is set. Does one character push the other on the swing? How does adding in a little description enrich the dialogue?

Script writer Jane Espenson says, "People get less articulate, not more, when they're emotionally moved. Want to write an emotional moment? Increase your quotient of stumbles and restarts."

Is this useful advice for you as you write?

Writing: 30 Minutes

When you're describing a place, the movement and actions of a character in that place can reveal what the place is like. When a character has to push through a crowd, the reader sees and feels the crowd.

Now, imagine that you are the last person left in the world. Write up to 400 words describing the world as you wake up in it. Think about the description and what actions you/your character must take that show the reader what the world is like to be in now. Use the scenic elements we've discussed in the chapter to enrich your writing.

Taking It Further

While writing for young readers isn't always the space for a lot of interiority, it's still fun to practise.

1. Write a diary entry by a kid about a surprise. It could be Christmas, a birthday, an achievement, or something else—good or bad, depending on their age.

2. The character should use the "I" voice to help them be open and honest.

3. Now rewrite the same piece but as a scene in the third person (he/she voice). What do you need to change? How is it different? Did you miss description or dialogue when you wrote the diary entry? What did you learn from doing this?

4. To challenge yourself, now imagine a kid on a cruise ship (pick their age). They hear someone start screaming. Thinking about action and pacing (there's no time for the character to think/reflect/ponder), and giving us only one or two lines of description, write what the character does next in an age-appropriate (to the age group you want to write for) block of text.

How different is your piece written with action as the focus to your piece where you've been deeply interior? Remember, what your characters do keeps your story moving forward and reveals their personality. How is this different from showing what they think? What's age-appropriate for your ideal reader? More action or more interiority?

10

DRAFTING YOUR BOOK

Whether you've started writing regularly or found it difficult to commit, the most important thing to remember is that a first draft only needs to exist. It doesn't need to be perfect. It doesn't even need to be good. It only needs to honour the promise of the story that is trying to appear on the page. I'd love for you to take the leap now and write a draft of a book. Yes, just like that. Except, it will look like repetition. Day by day, show up to the page and write: if you're a picture book author, you still need to be writing regularly, even if you finish a draft in a day! In this chapter, we'll look at some of the things I've learned about how to draft, whether you're writing for very young readers all the way up to young adults.

I believe that writing happens in two stages. The first is the stage where you write the book for yourself. This is true, even if you intend ultimately to share the book with readers. This first draft is for you, a special shiny secret for you, and you alone. I'm good at writing first drafts. I've had to work at the editorial part, but that's the next stage, for the next chapter. It's important not to let that stage get in the way when you're writing your first draft.

My friend has three children and longs to get words onto the page. But she's inhibited by what would happen when the children read those words. One day. When we talked about this, we were sitting in my van outside her house, in the dark with snow all around. She's very beautiful, and she's full of stories and magic. But she doesn't write because she's too close to the second stage—she's editing before she's written. I urged her to write for herself now. Later, later, later we decide as writers if we want to edit to share our work with others—our children, our families, our friends. It's easy for me to say it, but it's very hard to close off the voice that whispers: *what would someone else think?*

The problem is that as writers, we want to control everything. And we absolutely must control *the story*. In fact, we're absolutely in charge of the words we get onto the page. But we can't control the responses we get. We can't even imagine them. Did I imagine that one day I'd see a gif of a teenager banging their head over and over and over and over (you get it) as their review of *Life on the Refrigerator Door*? Thank goodness I didn't imagine that. Did I imagine that same book would be made into a play in Paris, Latvia, Japan, Tahiti, and London? Nope. For sure, I did not.

We can't predict or control or even properly fathom what the response to our work will be. And if we bring that into the writing, into this stage, those quiet moments when we encounter the page and discover our best selves, then it makes writing even more challenging. I find this poignant line by Anne Frank inspiring: "I can shake off everything as I write; my sorrows disappear, my courage is reborn."

In this chapter, I want to share with you how I go about drafting a book and give you some ideas for what this part of the writing process looks like so you can flourish.

A lot of this advice is for those of you who are working on a manuscript that will take several days, weeks, or months to write. If you're writing a picture book, this is very different. Because what you do day in and day out is write the book once. You'll still do the repeated work that I'm about to recommend, at the repeated time, and certainly for the first few drafts keep yourself in this mysterious state of play and creativity. My advice is to write the book over anew *each time*. No need to look at the last version; just try it again. You'll give yourself several versions to play with, and you'll find lines that you love and words that surprise you, like the six magpies crossing the sky we're about to encounter.

MAGIC AND MOMENTS

Lots of people who want to write for children and young adults have children and young adults in their lives. This can mean that finding a writing window can be very difficult indeed. Whether young people are in your life or not, there are plenty of responsibilities that get in the way of writing. Take the pressure off and make the time window for your writing short, but repeated. Give yourself this time to write again and again (remembering that it's messy and imperfect and editing happens later). Through the simple act of repetition, each time you sit down you will trigger your brain back into the story that was lurking in the background through the hurly burly of your days. I know we've looked at goals, but I want to spend a little time on some extra techniques for the writing-a-draft stage.

I suggest to you that you write as regularly and as consistently as you can when you're drafting a book. I like to write every day, and I get up early, which makes me fractious and over-caffeinated and tired. But the words are uninhibited and my Inner Critic and worrier doesn't really have time to surface if I set my alarm and step into the inky mornings to write. I commit to either an hour a day, or 350 words a day, depending on the book and my mood. Often, I write far more words, but I rarely write for more than an hour at a time during this stage. If I write in the mornings, my children give me a natural stopping point by climbing on me in their pyjamas, then pushing my laptop away. That's usually an hour or so into the writing. Sometimes, when they arrive on my lap sweet and sleepy, I get frustrated. "I just have to finish my sentence," I say. Then I remind myself that Hemingway used to leave his sentences half-finished exactly so he would come back to the page and know where to pick up.

If my kids arrive as I've finished, I write a note to myself telling me what to work on next time I go to the page. The notes look like this:

Dex goes to the lake.

Or:

> Llama gets more stressed.

Or:

> Go back to chapter two and layer in so this last scene has texture.

As you can see, these notes don't make sense to other people. Nor should they. They are a tiny arrow for me for my next bleary morning, so when I sit down, I'm not casting my line into an empty body of water. Instead, I know exactly how to begin. Try Hemingway's half sentence or my little note technique for yourself as you draft.

THE SLUMP IN THE MIDDLE

Writing is hard work.

Really hard work.

I'm not trying to make any of you feel discouraged here. Precisely the opposite, in fact. I'm trying to bust the illusion that writing has to be easy to be any good. I want to dispel the notion that writers merrily sit back while the story just flows onto the page, line after perfect line, paragraph followed by perfect paragraph, plot slotting into place, characters fleshy and real.

Real writers find out pretty fast that you have to earn the good days.

This means that, yes, sometimes, some rare and gorgeous days, the words do cascade onto the page and everything is easy. But many, many writing days are challenging. The writer takes wrong turns. Every sentence feels stiff and awkward until there is nothing more to say. The story is wooden and downright dull.

On these terrible writing days, your mind starts to play tricks on you, telling you that it isn't worth writing the story at all, insisting you should give up.

Don't give up.

Believe me, those days when it's going badly are actually good for your writing. I know it sounds unlikely, but by accepting—even expecting—difficult writing days, you are growing and improving as a writer. Writing shouldn't be easy to be worth doing. In fact, what would be the point of doing it if it were easy all the time?

Your unique imagination and stories are worth the fight. They are worth the struggle and hard work.

Practically, there are two ways to deal with a challenging writing day:

1. Push through it. Allow yourself to write badly and get words on the page. You can always edit them later.
2. Walk away. I heard Martin Amis talk at a festival once, and he said that as he matured as a writer, he learned to walk away if the writing wasn't going well. Take a stroll, do some gardening, cook, whatever, but let your mind relax into solving the problems on the page. Come back refreshed and ready to write. But come back soon…

I tend to push through on the page. A good friend of mine walks away when she is struggling. Either way works—you'll have to figure out *what works for you*. Whichever way ends up being *your* way, remember that sometimes when you think you're at a dead end, you're not. You've only got to look at the situation differently to discover hidden doorways and paths to a stronger story. Every writer gets stuck at one point, and often for me it's in the middle. Usually, what I have to do is go back to the overall story at this point and see where I've gone wrong. Is my main character not the one I want to write about? What's the sticking point?

Or have I forgotten that I need to keep going, even when it's difficult? That first rush of words has run out, and still, I need to write.

Yesterday morning, while driving the children to school, I saw six magpies fly over the road. The kids and I remarked on it. We went over the childhood rhyme, trying to recall what six magpies signify, and decided it was either *for a wish* or *for something better*. And then one of my sons got angry and yelled about something unrelated, and I dropped them off at school, and it was immensely cold and we hugged goodbye and my day rattled on.

At six this morning, when I encountered the page, there were the magpies. Six of them flew across the road where the character was—in a very different moment in her life to mine. I'd forgotten about the magpies, and yet, there they were. If you trust yourself that your brain is building and playing with the story the whole time when you're not writing, you'll find your own magpies and magic when you come to the page.

You won't always feel like it.

There are a lot of notions that drift about that writers sit down and words pour from them and then they print that out and just like that: a book is ready. You've probably seen something like this in a movie or even read a story where this was the writer's life. Alternatively, you've seen the writer staring at a blank page, frustrated, screwing up pages and chucking them into the garbage, missing the can as often as they get those paper balls in.

Yet, the act is more quotidian than that. It's writing a sentence. It's writing the next one. It's not quite knowing what to put next, but knowing there's only an hour to get through. It's reaching 230 words and telling yourself that you only need 120 more and then this is done. And some days—the wonderful, hard-earned days—it becomes words pouring and story filling every recess, the time passing like sugar through a sieve, disappearing, and the world morphing into the scene you now inhabit fully.

You never know which type of day you're going to get, but you earn the "good" days with the "hard" days. Neil Gaiman in his MasterClass says something along the lines of how you can't tell *at all* when you get to the editorial phase and read it over which type of day it was. I love this, because it's so true. All the days, the repeated and patient act of writing an actual book, lead you to a manuscript that is complete.

Tips for When You Get Stuck

1. Keep showing up to the page, at the same time, in the same way. Be patient.

2. Ask where it's not sitting right with you. Is there something niggling at you on an earlier page? Have you taken a wrong course? I like to go back and

correct. I'm not editing, just changing the direction so I can find the story again.

3. Do I need to read over a book I love that's close but different to mine? How did that author navigate their story?

4. Can I make the events of the story more challenging? What can my character do right now to change where things are headed?

ENDINGS

At some point, you'll reach the end. It won't be the end of the *writing* of the book—that comes later, once you've gone through the editorial steps. But you will get to a point where you think: *I've said everything I need to say for now. I have gone through everything and now I'm done.* Some writers like to write toward a scene that they can see as the final one early on. They aim for it.

Some writers like to give themselves a deadline to work to, others have those deadlines imposed by publishers. I like to marry up the end of my book with a date and then that helps me stay honest with myself on the page. If I'm skipping out on my appointed writing time, then the looming finish date reminds me to get back into my seat. At least, I do that for contracted books. Often, with my other books, I surprise myself by suddenly finding myself at the end, as if I've turned the corner on a country walk toward a pretty village in the UK and found a lovely place to eat and put up my feet.

You may get to the end and see nothing but the things you want to change. Try to take a break because it's important to celebrate the small and big moments of your writing life, and finishing a draft is a big moment. You've accomplished something you wanted to do: you've written a book. It's not perfect. It's not actually even finished. But *this* draft is done, and that's amazing.

CHAPTER 10 EXERCISES

Practical Task

Carve out a set time every day to write your draft. Commit to it. My advice would be to put your phone away and push through when you feel distracted. Just add words at this stage. If you're writing a picture book, having a daily writing time is still useful, even as you may be rewriting the entire book each time you sit down, depending on how swiftly you can write.

Check in with yourself after one week:

- Have I showed up for my daily writing as I get this draft down?
- Do I need to tweak the time?
- Any other changes?

Then commit again for another week, until you've reached your final page (of this first draft).

Writing: 10 Minutes

Write a list of three things to say to your Inner Critic when it shows up. We looked at this in Chapter 1 when we talked about ideas, but now as you're drafting a book, your Inner Critic might loom large, telling you the book is no good, that you can't write, that you have nothing to say.

An example of three ready replies might be:

1. Thanks for the feedback. Can you come back when I'm editing? But be kinder when you reappear.
2. I don't have time for this now. I only have an hour.
3. Stop talking. Just, no!

Writing: 30 Minutes

Play and flow on the page. Write, write, write. You'll be editing next, but now's the time to get words onto the page to hone later. These five transition lines are here for you if you're not sure what you want to start the next scene with. Use them:

1. The next thing that happened was...
2. When the sun came up, it was pale and limp. *Character* did what...
3. It wasn't much later, but...
4. Opening the door, it was...
5. *Character* could not believe who was walking over...

Taking It Further

What I want you to do as you're writing your draft but you want to take it further is to take your recovery seriously. The space when you are not writing is really important. Think about how you're going to fill it. Likely, you'll be dealing with work and responsibilities, but how can you best use your downtime? If you're watching shows or online, you're letting other people's creativity into your writing space *even if you're not writing at that moment.*

How much time can you free up to do not much at all? Walk, look out the window, breathe…

PART 3

REWRITING

11

EDITING

For years, for me, editing was the slapdash part of writing, but I've come to understand that editing is where the actual writing happens: it's where the book becomes what the first draft has promised it could be. It's where all the work you've done as a reader comes into play, where you learn to listen to your own inner voice, trust your judgment. You learn to ask, am I satisfied by this? But that can take some practice. When I first started to learn to edit my own work, I was deeply beholden to what other people said. I would hand a draft to a reader (a friend or, sometimes, a paid editor) and ask for their feedback. What I was looking for was them to tell me that my book was good—that *I was good.*

It wasn't until my first picture book was edited that I understood conceptually what editing was really for, and it wasn't my edits that I learned from, it was my illustrator's. Let me explain. When my illustrator, Bethanie Murguia, sent in her first version of the images for *Violet and Victor Write the Best-Ever Bookworm Book*, I thought they were gorgeous. They were gorgeous. The editor over at Little, Brown Books for Young Readers thought so too, and had some suggestions. Those edits took Bethanie nearly eight months. The final version is spectacular. But it's also an iteration of what Bethanie shared before. It's just even more wonderful. What I learned from this is that edits help you find what you're doing and make it better. Just as Emma Hill says, "The first draft is black and white. Editing gives the story colour." The best way to know how to make your work stronger is for you to know it well yourself first.

You know what you like as a reader. What I want to teach you as a writer in this chapter is how to listen to your own work, how to improve it yourself so that you know it's good before you start to share it with others. There are some steps to take to be your own best editor. Interestingly, the first step of self-editing is to walk away.

THE BREAK

Initially, you write a book for yourself, spending time in the glorious, lovely, and secret place of your story. Then you decide if you want to share it with the world.

At this point you need to pause.

Before you begin to reflect on your work, taking a break from your book is actually the best thing you can do *for it*. I know the urgent feeling of wanting to fix a line, but taking a break for a few days, even for a few weeks—I take a month—is the strongest way to begin the next phase.

To get the experience of seeing the work anew, as a reader will, you need a little space first. Once you've taken a break, then you come back to the work, turning your manuscript into a book that others want to read. During your break, I advise that you read lots of other books aimed at similar aged readers, preferably with a similar genre if you're writing MG or YA. So, if you're writing YA fantasy, read five or six YA fantasy novels during your break.

Have a notebook on hand to jot down thoughts and ideas as you read. But leave your manuscript alone. If you're reading six picture books, I'd advise you to make notes on thoughts you have about page breaks, pacing, and beautiful words, but that you stay away from the actual text for at least a week, if not two.

Begin with some deeper thinking and developmental edits, then move forward word by word, sentence by sentence, to see if you think the work is accomplishing what you set out to do. This is the same for whichever age group you're writing for, although some steps look slightly different. For me, editing begins with developmental editing.

DEVELOPMENTAL EDITING

Developmental editing is big-picture editing: story, structure, character, themes, tone, voice. It can feel overwhelming, but reassure yourself that major edits happen for writers at all stages of their career, and they happen for all types of books for children.

Here are a few lines from a developmental editorial letter I received for a chapter book manuscript:

> Introducing a non-human character as an extension of the child's emotions or a stand-in for the child's emotions is not a bad idea. I think it can work, but I don't think it works here. The toy actually gave me anxiety. There's such a frenetic and chaotic energy coming from it that it actually put me on edge.

As you can see, this isn't a small editorial shift—this isn't a suggestion to change a line or move a paragraph, rather to think about the motivation and being of *an entire character*. I'm lucky in my writing career now to have editors at publishing houses who will read through my work and give me suggestions and ideas (although it doesn't always feel lucky!). But before I send manuscripts to editors at houses, I like to have done a lot of editorial work first now.

During a developmental edit, you're really thinking about how a reader will interact with your story. Ideally, during your break from your book you've moved to seeing your story as a reader will see it.

To best approach developmental edits with your book, there are a few different steps depending on the age of your intended reader and the type of book you've written. Whatever book you're creating, your self-editorial process will look like *questions*. This is because questions help you see possibilities. There's never a right answer with a book, remember, just new ways of looking at your manuscript to see how you can best serve it.

Developmental Edits: Picture Books

I think it's a good idea to take your text and put it into a dummy picture book on paper. This is a visual mock up to help you see the page breaks of the book.

Once you've put your manuscript into a dummy book, it starts to look and feel different. Read it through, read it aloud, and ask someone else to read it aloud to you: it's remarkable how a line that sounds good in your own voice suddenly has trips and stumbles as someone else attempts to read it aloud.

For both of my Violet and Victor books I made at least twenty dummy books. I'd make one, then sit with it for a few days, make notes, and then make another. Here are some of the questions that I asked myself as I read through. I hope these are helpful for you.

Overall

- What do I like or dislike?
- How is my structure?
- What is a reader looking to find out by reading this?
- How does my work fit with the conventions of the genre?
- How is the opening hook?
- How is the ending?
- Is too much happening?
- How do the page breaks feel?
- How is the pacing?
- When I get to the end of my book, is there an idea I could have now to make the book more original?

Character Development and Dialogue

- Are my characters well developed and age-appropriate?
- Do I care to know more about them?
- What do they want?
- What does the main character want and what do they get?
- Do my characters sound real when they speak?
- Does the dialogue drive the story forward or fill up space?

I've been lucky in my writing life to read a lot of picture books by emerging writers and something I notice is that many are very long. Something I check, in fact, is word count for picture books before I begin to read, and I bet editors at houses check this, too. I also notice a lot of missed opportunities to show what the character is thinking and feeling *with their actions*. As writers, often picture book authors forget how much the illustrations will bring so they have lots of description of the visual.

Here are three other issues that I see in picture book manuscripts:

1. Endings that don't have a feeling of an ending
2. Characters who don't have much energy or motivation, or who aren't age-appropriate; often these characters have indistinguishable names
3. Not enough attention paid to language, rhythm, and cadence; forced rhymes

My advice is to make a lot of notes and to plan to rewrite at least five versions of the manuscript. I'd advise a week at least between each version. Once you have the strongest draft you can, it will be time to bring in another reader, which I look at shortly.

Developmental Edits: Chapter Books, Middle Grade, and Young Adult

At this stage, if you've finished a draft of your book for this age group and taken a break, I'd recommend you print it out and then read through the book as a whole to see how it's working for you. Changing mediums like this, from screen to paper, can be a really helpful way for your brain to read the book as a reader instead of as the writer. Take a pencil and make notes not on the manuscript, but beside you, in a notebook. Try not to get caught up in line-by-line fixes, and instead use the questions below to think about your book from a distance before you dive back in.

Remember, you can cut entire chapters. Or consider rewriting the whole book in a different tone or voice. Everything is possible at this stage. The voice that interrupts and tells you the book is terrible and not working—that voice is not helpful. Try to ignore it, and remind yourself that you have many drafts to go and that each one will bring you closer to the book you want to finish. These questions will help you as you read. Answer those that are helpful to your manuscript.

Overall

- What do I like or dislike?
- Does this make sense?
- Am I bored?
- Is anything too silly?

- Is it repetitive?
- How is my structure?
- What is a reader looking to find out by reading this?
- Where might the reader fall out of the story because it's hard to believe?
- How does my work fit with the convention of the genre?
- How is the opening hook?
- How is the ending?
- Is too much happening?
- One chapter in, is enough happening?
- Does the plot move forward and keeps me engaged?
- When I get to the end of my book, is there an idea I could have now to make the book more original?

Character Development and Dialogue

- Are my characters well developed and age-appropriate?
- Do I care to know more about them?
- What do they want?
- What does the main character want and what do they get?
- Do my characters sound real when they speak?
- Does the dialogue drive the story forward or fill up space?
- Character Motivation—does the character's desire stay the same? If it changes, is the progression natural and does it serve the story?

Flow, Narrative Arc, and Structure

- Is the narrative driven by characters and actions or is the flow interrupted by backstory and information dumps?

- Narrative Arc—has the character found what they want?
- Have they faced their darkest hour?
- Is the ending a surprise or predictable?
- Have I stereotyped characters or plotlines?
- Chapter or Scene Order and Breaks—does the order of my scenes make sense?
- Does each scene *cause* future events?
- Are my breaks in the best, most compelling places?
- Is my heart telling me to make any major cuts? (Listen to that voice inside. It's probably right.)

I have a few other thoughts for manuscripts for specific age groups that might be helpful as you think through your book. These are thoughts that have come to mind as I read the work of emerging writers *and* my own books:

- **Chapter Books**: When I read chapter book drafts, I see a lot of old-fashioned childhoods or activities that don't feel relevant to today's kids (Dad reading the paper, Mom cooking breakfast). I find a lot of overly complicated sentences that forget the chapter book is designed for a reader coming to reading for one of the first times. Often there's a missed opportunity for a strong main character and the stories are lacking in action.

- **Middle Grade**: In MG, firstly there's a lot of confusion with the age categories for readers, and the main character is too old or too young for these readers. I see a lot of confusing world building, too, especially in MG fantasy. Often the writer wants to put in the whole world and every detail, forgetting that we want to get to know the character(s) in that world. This leads to too much backstory. Dialogue is a great way to move story forward, and I see it used in an unrealistic way as exposition instead of as kids would speak. (And there are often missed opportunities for humour.)

- **Young Adult**: In some of the YA I read, the main character is whiny, self-indulgent, too interior, or too focused on the past with not enough happening in the present. This can lead to heavy backstory, tropes, and exposition in dialogue. Thinking about how to make these characters real and vivid is so helpful. Be wary of characters flipping through time, looking in mirrors, and missed voice opportunities. A strong voice really helps define a YA manuscript. There are also the same problems of world building that I see in MG, too.

When you've considered as many elements as possible, leave your notes for a few days. Then schedule in time to get back to the page. It's time for a rewrite.

REWRITING

As I rewrite, I like to work chapter by chapter, addressing the big problems. I repeat this process a few times, draft by draft, before I move into line edits. I realize it's hard work, and can sometimes feel like you need someone else to tell you if you're doing it right or wrong. That stage will come, and soon you'll be asking a reader for input. But for now, take some time to strengthen so that when you do get feedback you aren't hearing something you already know deep down. Excavate and interrogate so that your manuscript is the best it can be.

This process requires patience. Take your time with it. I've learned to enjoy it, which didn't come naturally to me but has helped me as a writer so much. I like to work in ninety-minute blocks and I create checklists for myself to work through. Here is a list of some notes I had for myself editorially as I rewrote this book; these aren't quite line edits, but they are slightly less dramatic than some developmental edits can be:

Work To Do

- Title! What is best: Treasure? Wonderland by Alice (perhaps not as funny as I think?)
- Read over chapter 11 and separate out into different age groups
- Read over chapter 13—Add in social media and school visits and libraries?
- Review booklist
- Review exercises/rewrite and shape in the same fashion for each chapter (Time? Tasks? Type—reading/writing two levels/thinking)

LINE EDITING

As Roald Dhal says, "By the time I am nearing the end of a story, the first part will have been reread and altered and corrected at least one hundred and fifty times. I am suspicious of both facility and speed. Good writing is essentially rewriting. I am positive of this." You are probably seeing now how true this is! At this stage, you can start to ask yourself which sentences you want to hone and which paragraphs work better if you move them. This is when your reading skills come into play in a different way. Instead of asking what you like or dislike overall, you start to hear how each sentence sounds to you, and how you want to change it. You have to pay attention to every time you struggle to feel satisfied by a sentence until you feel satisfied. It's a lot of work, but as you're someone who loves words you'll find the work fulfilling and creative.

Ten-Point Line-Edit Checklist

To help you, here is a checklist for you to interrogate your work line by line:

1. **Dialogue**: Is it realistic? Does it sound natural when it's read aloud? Does each character sound like themselves? Have I tagged speech properly?

2. **Tense**: Is the verb tense consistent in the writing? If not, should it be?

3. **Voice**: Does the author intrude (that's when your voice talks over the character!)? Does the voice of the piece stay the same all the way through? Should it?

4. **Point of view**: Am I shifting from one character's head to the other's? Does that make the piece choppy? Should I try sticking with one point of view?

5. **Scenes**: Is each scene maximized? Does it need more description or less? More interior monologue or less? More action or less? More dialogue or less? Is there enough conflict in each scene? Does it start and end in a way that propels a reader?

6. **Characters**: Is each moment with the character true to who they are? Is there any extra shading to add or to cut?

7. **Chapter/page breaks**: Are they in good places? Are the chapters the length I want throughout?

8. **Setting**: Is my setting consistent? Is my world building powerful and vivid? Is there too much description making the flow baggy? Is my timeline clear?

9. **Paragraphs**: Does each paragraph break in a logical place? Does each paragraph progress from beginning to end?

10. **Language, spelling, and grammar**: Line by line, have I used the best word, the strongest verbs, the clearest and most beautiful language? Is there a better word? Use it. Check spelling and grammar one last time, too.

What this process looks like for me is a lot of reading, redrafting, and reading again. The editorial process isn't quick and doesn't need to be. Learning to love it, and to be patient, has been the best thing I've done for myself as a writer. Also, and perhaps this is the most important thing, while it's really hard to edit your own writing, it's very much a part of the process. Later on, you'll work with editors and copy editors who help you see what you couldn't see as you self-edited, but learning how to read your own work is fruitful. When you're just about ready to throw the book out the window, that's when it's time to bring in a reader.

FINDING A READER

Writing is a solitary job. You sit and stare at a computer screen or sheet of paper with *only* your characters as company. I say *only*, yet I find hanging out with my characters thrilling. I never feel lonely or bored. But eventually, after the long days of self-editing, I need to check in with other people (real people, I mean) and see if what I'm doing is working as well as I hope.

It may surprise you to know that before I send work to my editors at publishing houses, I get feedback from a close group of readers, one by one. Yes, this is after I've done the developmental work and the line edit work I've just described...

Most of my books have required a silly number of rewrites. The first few drafts I do alone, as I've explained. Then, and only then, do I reach out for a reader to see if they can give me some feedback or suggestions. If you'd like to try this, ask around and see if any of your friends or colleagues would like to read a draft. I believe that you only need one reader at a time to get the best out of this process.

Ask your reader to read the manuscript and then ask if they'll meet with you (in person or virtually). If it's a picture book, I ask them to read it out loud to me. When they do this, it's much easier for me to hear where the book works and where it's struggling, as we already looked at in the developmental edits for picture books.

Next, I ask the following questions, one by one, and make notes on their answers:

1. What did you think the book was about?
2. What were you reading to find out?
3. Where did you put it down?
4. What impression did you get of the main character? Of other key characters?
5. Did you get lost anywhere?
6. Did anything get confusing?
7. What was the reading experience like?
8. Was there anywhere you got bored?
9. What did you love?
10. Is there anything else you'd like to say?

Notice how the questions are not: *Is the book good? Do you like it?* Neither of these questions help me get to a finished manuscript. In fact, they take the conversation into a very unhelpful place. Any kind reader is going to just say yes to both of those questions, which doesn't give you anything to work with. Or they say no, or drift off like the traveller on the boat with me in Indonesia, and that can curdle any writing joy.

My first reader is sometimes my dad, sometimes my mum. Then I turn to a couple of good writer friends, one by one. Based on what they say, I take a break. Then I rewrite a draft. Then I ask the other one to read it... And I redraft.

Then I go for more feedback. This time I send the project to a friend who is a teacher and also to a kid who I trust. During the pandemic, I asked ten kids to read a chapter book for me and give me their notes. Some of my readers (including those kids!) give careful, considerate edits written on the page as either line edits or structural comments. All of them bring something to the table. I gift them suppers or a book or flowers, and always my thanks!

In a later draft (I redraft carefully before using all my readers up), I get Yann to give it a read. I have also read all of Yann's books over the last twenty years as an early reader, sharing the editorial insights that I have. We've both learned not to try to *write* each other's books but instead to give feedback as a reader. Some of my readers just say nice things—every writer needs those people. Some are very good at spotting all the parts that need work (uh, Yann!).

So, here are my tips for dealing with feedback from readers so you can make your work the best it can be:

1. I've said this already in this chapter, but I do think it helps: before you ask for feedback, read through your work. There's no point in getting feedback on something you already know how to improve. If you can see something that needs fixing, then fix it first. It's the things you can't see that you want your readers to help you spot.

2. Choose which readers to listen to. Sometimes readers have good intentions but the feedback they give is unclear or hard to implement. If they say "this is

really good/bad/boring," it's impossible for you to do anything with that. Those readers mean to be helpful, but it's okay just to smile politely and move on to someone more constructive. The editorial questions I shared should help with this.

3. Be wary of feedback that is so critical it makes you feel like giving up. If getting feedback is making you feel like your writing is worthless, pull back until you find your creative spark. One super negative comment can leave you reeling—trust me, I know. But it shouldn't derail you. That reader isn't necessarily right. There are many books in the world that have sold many copies that some readers love and others hate—reading is an individual experience and it may be that the reader you've chosen isn't right for your book.

4. Notice that some readers hone in on line edits whereas others are good at giving big-picture ideas. You need both types of reader to get your work to the next level.

You're allowed to feel completely overwhelmed and exhausted by all these steps. Remember, use what's helpful to you and your process. If you've been sending work out for years and getting rejections, notice where you could add in an editorial step that might help you achieve your goals.

And if all this feels like something you'd like to skip, that's okay, too. I feel like that often. It's a struggle to get to the edits sometimes, especially when a new and shiny idea calls me instead. However, there is one more step to think about editorially and then this chapter is through!

HIRING AN EDITOR

There are some extraordinary editors online who are available for a fee to read your work and give you feedback. Before you decide to invest, you might want to connect with a local writer in residence (Saskatoon Public Library offers this, so check with your local library), or with an evaluation program with a writers' guild, like The Saskatchewan Writers' Guild, who absorb most of the cost so you can get excellent feedback more affordably. It can be very expensive to hire an editor, and I would recommend following all the self-editing steps carefully before shelling out.

If you decide you want to work with an editor, make sure you've found someone who you respect and trust. Review what they offer online, watch any videos they share, and read through the testimonials they have from other writers. See if they'll meet with you for a short chat before you start work so you can get a sense if the relationship is comfortable and feels safe. Expect to send them a portion or all of your book and then anticipate a wait of a few weeks, depending on the length and complexity of your book, before you get written notes. I would look for someone who includes at least one conversation with the written notes so that you can review their comments and then have time to meet with them.

Working with an editor is an opportunity for you to listen, either to their written notes or preferably to them speaking, too. Often as writers, we use the precious editorial moments to explain to the editor what you were trying to do, but it's much more useful to listen and make notes. My advice to is try to ignore the defensive inner you who wants to protect your words, and give yourself time to absorb their feedback: make notes and ask for a recording of the call to watch after. It may not be that you incorporate all their advice, but hearing it is the first step.

Phew, we're through the editorial chapter. As you can tell, you can spend weeks and months on this part of the process. Because next is sending work out into the world...

CHAPTER 11 EXERCISES

Practical Task

The practical task for this chapter is to take a break. Actually! If you're tempted to get back to the book too soon, read this quotation over to yourself and see if it has a truth that applies to your work:

> "Taking a break can lead to breakthroughs."
>
> —Russell Eric Dobda

Now, think about how you're going to use the time away from your book. Which books could you read during a writing break?

Writing: 10 Minutes

Sometimes when I'm editing, I like to maintain a writing practice. I use prompts to write for short bursts so I have possible material for the next book. If this excites you, try it: Free-write about a kid who is lost (you choose their age).

Writing: 30 Minutes

Read over the questions I've shared with you in this chapter. Take one or two and adapt them to be useful in your own work. Now make some written notes on your manuscript. The main part of the exercise will be to slow down and take thirty minutes on the notes. Remind yourself to please your own ear first before you race to please anyone else's.

Taking It Further

How are these two quotations applicable to your work? Even for writers of long YA novels, the notion of where to cut is interesting and challenging. Read over both quotations and think about how they could impact your writing.

> "Let's put it this way: if you are a novelist, I think you start out with a 20-word idea, and you work at it and you wind up with a 200,000-word novel. We, picture-book people, or at least I, start out with 200,000 words and I reduce it to 20."
>
> —Eric Carle

> "So the writer who breeds more words than he needs, is making a chore for the reader who reads."
>
> —Dr. Seuss

Next, I'm sharing with you some editorial notes from my short hi-lo novel *Dropped*! A hi-lo book is aimed at reluctant readers and so has specific word counts and chapter lengths. Read through these edits and think about how you'd approach comments similar to this in your own writing. How does pacing impact your book? How about character motivation?

PACING/STRUCTURE

- You grab the reader's attention right away and jump straight into the heart of the story, which works so well both for a hi-lo and for this story specifically.

- I really liked how you set each day as a separate chapter. Normally I'd leave that as is, but for the Anchor, we like to have about 8–10 short chapters (generally around 750–1,000 words), which make it easier for reluctant readers to follow. I suggested dividing each day into 2–3 chapters. I suggested the location of the breaks based on both word count and where the plot either changes or becomes cliff-hanger-y.

CHARACTERS

- In your original outline, Dex is described as having been really popular in person, along with a huge online presence, before he ruined his social life. I didn't really get that from the manuscript. It's clear that he had a certain image online and that he had a girlfriend and friends (who ended up being crappy). But he doesn't come across as having been Mr. Popularity. Is this what you were going for?

- I think it would be helpful to strengthen his motive for going on the show and wanting to win. We know that he wants Lola to be watching and that he wants to win her back. But near the beginning of the book, he talks more about the contest as being a way to escape from his life and from being an online failure, rather than a way to regain his popularity/status.

- I noted in the manuscript that it would be great to elaborate a bit on Dex's mom's relationship with social media, as a way to give more insight into Dex's need for it.

12

WHAT HAPPENS NEXT?

Remember how I mentioned celebrating your successes as a writer. If and when you complete an edited draft of a book, then please remind yourself that this is a huge accomplishment. If you have a finished manuscript, edited and splendid, and you've celebrated that massive success, you now have a couple of questions to consider.

THE NITTY GRITTY OF TRADITIONAL, HYBRID, AND SELF-PUBLISHING

In this era of publishing, it's both very, very easy to publish and very, very hard. It's entirely up to you as a writer how you share your work with others. You may decide to put the work in a drawer now, and never let anyone else read it again. That's valid, but don't make that choice because you're intimidated by what sending work out in the world looks like.

If you'd like to publish your book, there is one big choice that you get to make, and then, once you've made it, a bunch of smaller choices that follow. I want to give you advice and tools to help you regardless of which choice you make.

The big choice: do you want to have a traditional publisher publish your work or would you rather self-publish?

Here are some things to consider as you make this first big choice.

THE TRADITIONAL ROUTE

The traditional route goes something like this: write your novel or picture book. Send sample chapters of your novel to an agent or a publisher. You can find who is currently looking for work many ways. I love the subscription magazine that *Children's Book Insider* sends by email with Above the Slushpile codes and advice from agents and publishers. A slushpile is an industry term for a pile of manuscripts that have been sent to publishers in hopes of finding a home. Eventually someone in the industry asks to see the whole book. A gatekeeper has finally accepted it. If that's an agent, then you work on edits together, and then the agent sends the book to publishers.

The reality is that many large publishers will only accept manuscripts from agents, so you have to approach agents first. If you want to approach publishers first, here in Canada, there are a few publishers who accept un-agented or unsolicited submissions. It's worth doing some research and asking around, and I've made some suggestions in the resources chapter, too.

Hopefully, a publisher accepts the manuscript. If there are to be illustrations, they begin the search for an illustrator. Maybe two years later, your book arrives in the world. Yes, you read that right. It's a slow process. When you go this route, the publisher takes on the financial costs of the book, including illustrations, editing, design, printing, sales (both getting your book into stores and libraries, and shipping), and some marketing and publicity. These costs can be significant for the publisher depending on the length and complexity of your book, as well as the number of books to be produced (the print run). As the author, you are paid an advance (which is a set fee, often half when you sign the contract, and half when you hand in the finished and polished manuscript, because the in-house editors will be making suggestions). Once you've earned out your advance, meaning the sales have covered your advance and the book is now earning money above and beyond that, you can then earn royalties, which may be in the region of 10 to 15 percent of the sale of a copy of the book. If you don't ever earn out the advance, you don't have to pay that back.

It's complicated. As this has always been the route I have been on, I've worked with an agent who helps me navigate the contracts, sends the work to publishers for me, and negotiates terms and rights. This route has meant I've worked with some incredible editors, illustrators, and teams. It's also meant that for twenty years I've been dealing with rejection: I still get rejections, and I'll come back to this shortly as it's an important part of the writing process. First, let's look at the world of self-publishing.

SELF-PUBLISHING

Self-publishing is split into two main areas. Either you do all the work yourself, or you work with a hybrid publisher. I suggest a couple in the resources at the back of this book. If you do all the work yourself, you will be in charge of editing, cover design, printing, marketing, and making sure your book gets into the hands of readers. You also bear the financial costs, and, in turn, receive all the money that the book makes.

Some writers are amazing at all the roles required to publish a book. Other writers subcontract parts out (like the cover design). I have limited advice on all of this because I've never self-published, but I do recommend you head immediately to Arthur Slade's website, which is full of amazing insight (he both self-publishes and publishes traditionally).

I worked with a hybrid publisher called Your Nickel's Worth Publishing when my partner Yann worked on a book with them for a friend of his. I've also done some editorial work for some of their beautiful kids' books. They work with editors and copy editors (checking that your grammar and punctuation is perfect). They organize and complete the book design (which can be very complicated with an illustrated book—if you're self-publishing you get to choose your illustrator). They know about paper and covers, and they help with distribution. If you want to explore this route for your journey more, I have recommendations for you at the back of this book. Do make sure to take time with the research if this is your path so that your dream to have a published book isn't exploited. There are always unscrupulous companies looking to make money from your work. There are also amazing and generous companies that help you make your dream of a beautiful book a reality.

7 Questions to Ask Yourself as You Decide

There are as many reasons to seek a traditional publisher as there are reasons to self-publish your work. Research both thoroughly to make sure you have as much information as possible. I've never self-published anything, so I'm not an expert in this area, but these questions cover the main areas for you to help you make your decision. Sit with the following seven questions:

1. Which most appeals to you? Your answer here will come from your heart. Listen to it.

2. Do you want creative control over design, layout, illustration, and marketing? If you do, consider heading along the self-publishing/hybrid route.

3. Can you keep writing if you get rejected? Do you see those rejections as opportunities to improve your writing? If rejection feels manageable to you, then you will be robust enough to handle the risk of sending work to traditional publishers and agents. If you've tried sending work out and received rejections, you may feel self-publishing is your only option. That's fair, but (as I explore below), rejection sometimes suggests to me that my book needs another draft: that may be true for you whether you decide to send it out again or self-publish.

4. Are you good at contracts and business? Self-publishing is a whole business, and many writers excel at not only the writing but also the business side of this work. Knowing your answer to this will help you see which route you want to take.

5. Do you want your book out quickly? If yes, then self-publishing could be the route for you. The book's production process still takes time in either route, but your personal timeline isn't tied to a seasonal schedule in the same way it is for a traditional publisher. Racing to get a book out isn't always the *best for the book*. Traditional publishers add your book to a complementary list of other books that can help sell your book. It will be part of media and marketing campaigns that help your book be discovered.

6. Do you have money to put toward the creation of your book? Self-publishing can become very expensive: a book can cost from $5000–$25,000, but for some writers this investment is worth it. If this route pulls you, you can seek a grant, funding, or turn to crowdsourcing. Depending on where you live, there may also be local or national arts councils that have grants you can apply for.

7. Are you comfortable going out selling your book, to make sure that bookstores and librarians know about it? While traditional publishers will still ask you to

work on and be engaged in your own marketing and publicity, they will support this. Self-promotion is difficult and takes a lot of time and energy: even navigating the various social platforms to best share your book is challenging. If you're self-publishing, this will all be up to you. With traditional publishing, you'll get some help and support, although both ways you'll have to think about how to build your platform, which we look at very briefly in Chapter 13.

REJECTION

Now that you've had some time to think about the route you'd like to take, the rest of this chapter will be about how to send work out for traditional publishing.

But, before I talk more about how to send out work, I want to share a bit about what happens when you get a rejection. I want to do this now, because rejection can come at any stage after you've shared work with someone else. You could show your beautiful book to a friend or colleague, you could get feedback from a writing group or professional writer, or you could bravely send work to a competition or publishing professional.

Before I first published, I had a lot of rejections. Likely, you too will get rejected along the way. I don't say that as some ghastly soothsayer, creating a future that now will come true. I say it because if you don't get a rejection letter or feel rejected at some point, then you're a writer unicorn!

My first rejection letter was the beginning of a flood of rejection that began twenty-five or so years ago. I remember the wording: *Thank you for your submission. We're sorry but…*

Worse, and it does get worse, the rejection letter was accidentally sent to the wrong address, to a different writer who was also rejected, so she called up to inform my mother of my rejection. *Hi, I'm calling to let you know that Alice Kuipers' novel was rejected.* Worse even than that was the gentle, sad tone of my mother. *I'm sorry, sweetheart, they rejected your novel.* For a first-time rejection, it was a triple whammy of YOUR BOOK FAILED YOUR BOOK FAILED YOUR BOOK FAILED.

Or maybe, if I'm more honest, the nasty little voice inside was actually saying: *You failed, you are a failure, you will always fail.* I took a gin and tonic and collapsed in front of bad TV. (Everyone finds their own way to cope.) My book had been humiliated by the agency, the other writer, my mother. No! *I* had been humiliated by them all. Humiliation has a bitter taste, so gin and tonic was ideal to swallow it down. Bitter on bitter. I would quit writing forever.

Actually, I quit writing for a few days. I sat around getting jittery and grumpy and realized I was going to have to sit down with words on the page again, even though I'd had a rejection letter and even though I was a failure. (This is my own internal monologue—I don't think anyone who gets a rejection letter is a failure. I actually think they're brave for sending work out into the world.)

Then I sat down and wrote something else because writing makes me feel better, and I needed to feel better. Writing helps me understand the darker thoughts, it helps me turn them into story, and it soothes me when I'm sad. What else was I going to do in the face of feeling so low other than write?

I took some time before I sent work out again, but I *did* send work out again. No matter how normal it is, it's still difficult twenty-five years and many published books later. It's just a part of the process.

The rejection deluge began. One afternoon, I gathered three rejection letters from my mail-slot. They added to the other four I'd received that week. Seven rejection letters in one week. I slipped on the top step, and the rejection letters and I tumbled to the ground. It was a moment of humiliation, sure. But also, a moment of illumination because I knew, despite my pathetic situation, *I still wanted to write.*

Writing books requires a certain delusion, especially if you want to publish traditionally. The delusion is that someone else wants your story. A belief that it's worth doing even when no one ever reads it. A few days after the seven-rejection-letters-plus-sprained-ankle episode, my first novel sold. It's published in lots of countries, and it has won awards. The same with my second and third novels, and beyond. And yet, I *still* get rejection letters. Every letter *still* makes me feel horrible. But, soon after, it makes me feel like working harder. I had the most brutal rejection letter of my career as I was writing this book. The issues were so global for this particular editor that the first line of her letter to me was: *This book is not a winner*. I read it to Yann and he said, *Wow, I'd just give up if I got a letter like that*. Except it isn't true. He's had his share of rejections, too, and he hasn't given up either. Writing is essential for both of us because it makes us *who we are*, and it's how we understand the world.

Whatever form of response to my books, whether from a fan or a detractor, I'm still the writer lying on the grass at the bottom of the steps, rejection letters scattered around me, ankle hurting like crazy. Every single book I begin, I feel the same sense of terror and excitement. The same delusion. Every single time I know I must put everything I have into the book. It's exhausting. It's exciting. It's a risk. A painful, thrilling risk. I'm totally addicted.

Not to the rejection. I'm addicted to the writing in the same way I'm addicted to reading. I'm sitting as I write this with my kids doing parkour, calling to me: *Mom, watch!* and I *still* have the peace within that writing affords me. Writing helps me step back and it helps me dive in, all at once. While I'm glancing over at their shenanigans in the gym, I'm also writing this to you, and I'm remembering those rejection letters, and the many other moments of humiliation and joy that writing has afforded me.

Those of you who are reading every word here will have noticed that I mentioned twice that I still get rejection letters. I had one this week. It was from an editor who I admire, for a book I feel works fantastically, and it's taken her nearly six months to get back to me. If I had any writing ego left, it would have suffered those six months. Instead, I've learned to take the rejection I get and use it to fuel me to look at my work from a new perspective. Sure, I think this book is fantastic, but the editor absolutely does not. My opportunity at this point is to ask myself *how could it be better?*

I feel the sting of the criticism, sure. I'm not made of stone. But once my ego has stepped out of the way, I can use what she says to review the material fully and perhaps decide I want to make the book the best it can be. Or I realize that this beautiful book of mine, the one I wrote and loved and edited and re-read a thousand times, might never be a book that anyone else wants to read. Once I've had time to go through her comments, I'll know that I've given it everything I have and that whatever happens with the book in the world, it's taught me to be a better me.

ABANDONING

I know, I know. I still haven't got to how to query, but I think it's helpful to pause a little before sending work out. There's one other risk to rejection letters, and it's a major one. I want you to pause and read this before you learn how to query and open yourself up to that risk. A rejection letter or ten might lead you to abandoning your work. I really don't want the outside world to crush your writing life.

Some writers, and I include myself in this group, abandon projects. And some never do. Some writers abandon projects for good reasons, and others because someone else has told them they don't want their book. I'll share what abandoning looks like for me, and give you some tools to navigate those feelings yourself. And then I'll share with you some tips for those brave moments when you do write your query letter.

I have a low tolerance for boredom, and I'm not patient with my work. Sometimes I read through edits and notes and realize that while the editor is right, I *don't want to do the work* to make the book or story better. Because this happens to me multiple times a year, the process of abandoning a book is one I know well. The writer Elizabeth Sims recommends asking yourself a lot of questions before you abandon a book. I ask myself questions, too: If I just worked harder, if I followed through until the book or story was complete, if I did that, then would the finished book be worth it?

I think this is a good way to look at it. For me, if the answer is yes, the book would be worth it, absolutely. The other question is: do I want to keep going? Maybe, like me, you have to account for your personality and tendency to chase the new. Sometimes, for me, even if a book is worth it, I still don't want to keep going.

When the answer is no, I sit with it a little. I check that it's not just a frustration or a whim. And I triple-check I'm making the decision for *me*, not because of what I believe someone else thinks. And then, I let go.

Sometimes, actually, I abandon a book halfway through—these projects never get sent to editors, they never get read by anyone else, and they sit in my hard drive, never to be seen again.

But more often, I quit at the editorial point. I get the rejection letter and I suddenly see that the book or story can't ever be what I want or need it to be. I see something profoundly unfixable in the text, and so put it to one side.

This is not fun.

When it happens, it's hard. I aim to write books and stories that I at least finish before I give up. Yet, still, I give up. I'm contemplating giving up a book I've been working on for three years right now. *And that's okay.*

These are hard places for a writer to go. And I do not recommend that you abandon books and projects as frequently as I do. I have a high attrition rate, but I also write a *lot*. I have seven or eight stories or longer texts that I've given up on this year alone, but I'm grateful to each and every one of them for what they've taught me. And, at the same time, I have five books that are coming out that I've written this year. Three with my name on them (two are books for kids and one is this book for you). Two belong to their authors now (I ghosted for them).

All this to say, sometimes it's the right decision to abandon a manuscript and sometimes it's the wrong decision.

These further questions will help you decide what's right for you:

1. Are you putting the book to one side because someone else told you it wasn't worth it in some way (rejection, dismissal, disinterest, destructive criticism)?
2. Are you putting this book down because you don't know where to send it?
3. Are you putting these words away, even though they still matter to you, because you believe no one else cares?

If any of these answers are yes, then I think you could pause before abandoning the project. It may feel hopeless at this point, but it may not be the end of the road. Erica Jong says, "I went for years not finishing anything. Because, of course, when you finish something, you can be judged." If your reason, deep down, is that the judgment of others is holding you back, I think that you should give your book another chance.

Because I don't think anyone else can end the story for you. If you want to talk about the book, and you have a tiny fire inside that you can reignite by closing the door to the outside world and getting back to the page, then please go light that fire. Don't let your Inner Critic and damaged confidence rule you.

Now answer these questions:

1. Are you pulled by a new idea?
2. Are you wanting to write something different?
3. Are you impatient to get that feeling of flow back into your life, the one you get when you're faced with a blank page and the words come?
4. Are the edits/feedback very challenging (although not insurmountable)?

These are harder questions. The pull of the new is always strong for me. It's easier for me to begin a new project than it is to do the editorial work required on an old one. Usually, if these are the questions I'm answering yes to, I know I have to schedule in time with the manuscript I'm trying to drop. I'm trying to get out of doing the work, but if I do it, then it will be worth it. Likely, it's the same for you.

This final set of questions are useful, too:

1. Does the idea of talking about the book or story with someone else make you feel weary or bored?

2. Has the book or story taught you something you didn't know before? Do you feel in a new place and ready to walk on with what you've learned, but unwilling to spend time connecting with that story anymore? You've learned all it can teach you, say?

3. Have you seen that this particular project doesn't work *in your own view*? Not that someone else has told you it doesn't, but that the icky feeling

> that there's something insurmountable that your own inner voice has been muttering has got loud enough for you to hear? Triple check this isn't your Inner Critic. There's a difference between that and your gut, but it can take some practice learning which is which.

If the answer is yes to these three questions, then maybe it is time to take a break. Or abandon the book. It may be that you come back to this project later—it's always there. I don't suggest you delete it, just put it to one side and wait until you feel like reading it again one day. So, now we've dealt with the darker side of sending work out, let's move into some concrete advice for you on how to get your gorgeous, shiny book into the hands of traditional publishers. You're going to want to do a lot of research and perhaps even create an excel document to help you see where you've sent something and what the response was.

AGENTS

An agent represents an author, sending work out to publishers for you. Your agent takes a commission from any money you receive—including advances and royalties—but deals with all the complexities of contracts, helping you navigate the rights you're selling to a publisher.

If you want your book to be published by one of the larger publishing houses, then you'll need to find an agent to represent what you've written. Lots of publishers won't read work unless it's submitted by an agent, meaning there is one more layer of gatekeeping between you and your work being a published book.

Agents take a percentage of anything you earn, but do not charge you anything. Often newer writers forget that an agent works for you, and will love your work. My agent is a sounding board and my relationship with her has been going on for fifteen years or so now. I respect her, treat her professionally and with gratitude, and I listen to her advice. When she loves my writing, she tells me. When a book doesn't work for her, then she lets me know. I trust her, and I want you to work with someone who you trust, too.

Tips to Find an Agent

Research agents who work with authors you admire. You can either use the internet, or the books you've recently read and loved, to find out who your beloved authors are agented by. Follow these agents online and notice what they are seeking to read.

Network to meet possible agents and publishers at conferences in person, or do this online, too. There are webinars and opportunities to connect with the industry if you stay patient, polite, and professional. Once you get a sense of a few names, then it's time to send out query letters.

If you're writing picture books or chapter books, submitting directly to a publishing house might be the better route, especially as you start. Agents don't always seek these books and so direct submission is often accepted at those publishing houses.

Whether you are sending work to an agent or decide to go directly to a publishing house, the next step is querying.

QUERYING

Agents and publishers receive a lot of query letters, and it can be difficult to get your work noticed, read, or accepted. Firstly, researching publishing lists and comparative titles helps you discover agents or publishers who will be interested in your book. Sending a YA horror to an agent or publisher who loves biographical picture books, for example, is a waste of time for both the publisher and for you, delaying response times and increasing the chances of a rejection. All of this research is easy to do online, and many agents and publishers share their desired next books on their social media and websites. One thing to keep in mind is that if you're writing in English, for example, you're not limited to publishers or agents in your home country. You can submit to British, Canadian, American, or Australian agents and publishers, too. If you're writing in other languages, you can submit to any agent or press that works in that language.

Once you've found some possible options, fully pay attention to what the agent or the publishing house asks for in an ideal submission package. Maybe they want the first three chapters, maybe they want just one. Likely they want a synopsis, but should it be one page or two? Make sure you follow the unique requirements of where you're sending your work. Getting this right will give you a better chance of your work being read than the other gazillions of writers out there, but it doesn't offer any guarantees. This side of writing, the industry and business side, can be very challenging and can require a lot of patience. Remind yourself that this will all take time, and try to carve that into your calendar.

Whether you are querying an agent or a publisher, remember to stay professional—think of sending your work out as a job interview on the page. Your book is the one looking for the job.

As you prepare your submission package, two parts often befuddle newer authors. Firstly the query letter and then the synopsis. Your query letter is the first thing that your new agent or editor sees, and it has to cover a lot of ground quickly: it needs to showcase you, describe your book, and tempt the editor to begin reading your synopsis and chapters. Each query letter needs to be tailored for each possible connection. Keep it professional and polite. Make sure your query letter has a salutation and an introductory comment that shows you've paid attention and done your homework. Writing to an agent who has never represented young adult fiction and who doesn't like it, with your YA work, doesn't bode well. Remember, this is like a job interview done on the page—this is the first time anyone at the agency or house is reading your words. Make each sentence relevant, polite, and error-free. Agents and publishers love books and words. That's why they do the work they do. Typos and lack of clarity will be annoying to them. Remember, the first time they are reading any of your work is in this query letter. Why would they read pages of your book if you can't demonstrate that you can write a letter?

A key part of a query letter is being able to sum up what your book is about quickly. This is known in the industry as the elevator pitch. Imagine you're in an elevator and you have thirty seconds to describe your book to a publishing professional. It can take time to write this pitch, so it's worth writing it a few times and even testing it out with friends. From your pitch, you'll be able to shape your synopsis.

Your synopsis is a description of what happens during your book, summing all the key plot points. Often, newer authors want to hold back surprises so as not to spoil the story, but an agent or publisher wants to know exactly what they are going to be reading.

In the exercises at the end of this chapter, we'll dive deeper into this.

Query Letter and Submission: Final Tips

1. Make sure that you're clear in your cover letter as to what your book is about, and who it's for. Test run your hook line and your synopsis before you send out your work. See if others understand what your book is about, or if they're puzzled.

2. Remember that agents and publishers read a lot more submissions than they are able to represent. Often, they want to be able to say yes, but they have to navigate a lot of authors. Be patient and try not to let your self-worth and your love of your book be diminished by slow or non-existent responses.

3. Revise your letter/hook/synopsis several times before you send it.

CHAPTER 12 EXERCISES

Practical Task

Think of your elevator pitch as the one or two lines that you'd say to someone if you only got to talk to them briefly. Your description of your book should include your character, the setting, and what your character is up against. Take some time to research online how other people write a two-line pitch for their book.

Writing: 10 Minutes

Write an elevator pitch for your book. Just do it. You will edit this lots and lots later!

Writing: 30 Minutes

A query letter requires that you share with your dream agent or publisher your book and a bit about you, and that you do it all professionally, politely, and with no typos! Search online for tips on writing a great query letter and then use your thirty minutes to draft one today.

Taking It Further

A synopsis is a full description of your book. You won't need to do this if you've written a picture book: if you're writing a picture book, your task is to look up how agents and publishers expect a picture book manuscript to be formatted when you send it in.

For those of you with longer manuscripts, it's time to write a synopsis. Here are some tips:

1. Keep it focused on the character and what happens to them.

2. Don't hold back the interesting parts: agents and editors want to see exactly what the book is about.

3. Research online how others have written theirs, and see which ones you like best. Check with the agent/publisher that you are sending to exactly how they'd like this document to be. Submission guidelines are usually posted on a publisher's website. Some want one page, others want two, for example. Again, remember that you can edit your synopsis, and likely you will several times. You can read it over to a friend and see what they notice, too.

13

YOUR WRITING LIFE

A writing life isn't just sitting and putting words on the page: it has a lot of elements to it. As Leo Tolstoy says, "The two most powerful warriors are patience and time." Your writing life will involve writing, but the time when you're not at the page is often where the story unlocks. When you're not at the page, your work is opening up in your mind. You're thinking and developing your work as you wash the dishes, say. Well, that's what I remind myself!

But, as well as thinking, a writing life has various other pieces that impact your creativity and ability to reach your goals. Connecting with readers is very much part of a writing life for authors: your platform and in-person talks are both key. Another part of a writing life is how to navigate the ebb and flow of confidence and how to manage when life gets in the way of your writing.

All these parts of your writing life, if and when they come into play, will require juggling and learning. My writing life looks like writing regularly, sure. But it also has many other moving parts, and I want to share a bit of some of them to help you with your own writing life.

Usually, I wake and read before I get out of bed. Some mornings, if I'm working on a first draft, I'm awake early and writing before I even have time to think. Other mornings, I coach writers or read. Then there's (coffee!) the kerfuffle of the school run before I walk or workout (on an ideal day). My workday begins after all that, and I break it into ninety-minute blocks, as I explained in the chapter on flow: the first time block is for a new draft, edits, or re-reading my manuscript. Often, the second block is for that, too. Afternoon blocks are where I focus on connecting with readers: school visits, social media, my Substack (which I love; please come and find me there!), admin (invoicing, emails, blurbs for other writers), or any classes I'm taking (I love online classes). After I pick up my kids, I use broken time blocks to manage all their needs (hockey registration, driving them, making food), before making some time to read before bed.

In this chapter, we'll look in more depth at some of these elements so you can figure out how to incorporate them into your writing life. Likely, you'll have a job or other responsibilities that take up a lot of your time, but now we're going to work on putting writing elements into your days. My advice for anyone is to write your book before adding in the other elements. Put writing in your primary time block (after your actual job is done, of course!).

SOCIAL MEDIA AND YOUR PLATFORM

As a writer for children and young adults, you'll likely want an online platform, including a website and current social media.

Crafting a good social media presence and writer platform takes time and energy. I like to think about it, after advice from both T-Squared Social and Kelly Weekes, as writing a message to one person. That helps me remember I'm not writing to everyone, and that I only need to focus on how to write something that this one person can enjoy. Create a character who you're writing for, if you like, and focus your message for them.

I enjoy the online elements that connect best for me. I love Substack and so use it as a newsletter that copies to my blog. I like making videos and I'm comfortable chatting online about the books I've read and how they help me write. My advice is to see what you enjoy and, as you'll try in the exercises, find a writer you love online and learn from them. Take what's useful for your writing life and begin. Just like with writing anything, you are free to play and make mistakes. The idea of making a mistake on social media is terrifying because of the loud backlash, but unless you're behaving egregiously, you can test out what works for you. For a while, I made word games because I love them so much. They weren't getting much traction, and although I enjoy making them, I'm now using my online time differently. In this way, I test out what works and what I love, finding a middle ground. Ultimately, at the heart of what I do online, I remind myself that I'm sharing to help other people. I enjoy engaging with and promoting other writers. Building this community gives me a place to talk books, have fun, get inspired, and keep my focus outward. When I'm promoting a book, I can lean into the people I've built relationships with to see if they want to read it, and when they're sharing their work, I can be part of getting the word out. I focus on engagement instead of follower numbers: what conversations do I want to have today? Find me online and read my Substack if you want to spend more time with me and see how I do all of this.

LIBRARY AND SCHOOL VISITS

Another part of writing for children and young adults is presenting your work to kids at libraries and in school. These visits can be a magical part of the job. I love encountering kids, talking to them, seeing them focus and listen, and at the same time I find myself really tired when I've been doing a lot of time with classrooms.

I remember when I first had to do a school visit and I was standing in front of over 300 kids, and the teachers *all left the room.*

At that point, I learned hyper-fast what kept kids interested and how to manage.

Now, I use visual presentation tools every time I do a talk (and I always show up early to make sure the tech is working well). I bring a lot of energy and joy to presentations. And I remember always, as I do with my online communication, that all my work in public is to help others. Kids want to learn about writing so they can tell their stories. They want to hear about my work *so they can create their own.* People online want to know tips and tools for their own lives. When I keep in mind the needs of the people I'm talking to, either online or kids in a school gym, then I do all of that work better and with more joy and less self-consciousness.

For now, I hope that little glimpse helps you navigate your writing life. Likely, you'll want to make time for submission or research into self-publishing; perhaps you'll want to add in a writing class or more time for reading. As you frame your writing in your mind as important to you, more writing-based activities will spill into your hours. So remember, always come back to the book you're writing. That's where you spend the best writing time!

PARENTING AND RESPONSIBILITIES

I was close to finishing this book when someone reached out to me on Instagram to ask me to write about how I manage to parent and work as a writer. The answer lies partly in the earlier chapter on goal setting and time management, but it also lies in a truth I return to over and over.

Writing makes me kinder. Which in turn makes me a better parent. I'm considerably grumpier if I don't write for a few days. There's no sense to it, but that's how I am. Prioritizing writing most days makes me nicer on all the days. My kids definitely prefer me when I'm nicer. As Yann knows well, I'm much, much, much nicer to live with when I'm writing lots.

The other thing I do remind myself of is that my kids fill me up with ideas when I'm not writing. Yes, I'm sure I've forgotten millions of words because I loaded my life up with children. But my children also get me excited about stories. Reading to them feels like a way of learning about the latest most amazing book written by an author for kids. Recently, Miriam Körner, a terrific author from Saskatchewan, sent her picture book *Fox and Bear* to us. I read it to my youngest sons, oh, forty times. They wanted it every day. Over and over. We spent ages looking at the gorgeous details in the pictures. We talked about the words, and I thought about how she artfully sets up the needs of the two characters. Would I as a writer, honestly, have read that beautiful book so many times without my children urging me to? I doubt it. Yet reading it forty times taught me new things about writing and structure. Her stunning book showed me a way to tell a story and brought magic into my life, and all of that was emphasized because my children took me away from writing my own books into a world where we read Miriam's book together.

When all the kids are puking and I'm sick and the house is a mess and it's been days since I've written, it's frustrating, yes. But I have to let go. I can't always meet the goals I set, and I can't always get to the page. So, I give myself grace, and I remind myself that when I do get to the page (which gets harder and harder the longer I'm away), I'll be less likely to snap at the kids or feel resentful at the endless domestic to-do list. Sometimes, I turn on all their screens just so I can write. Other times, I take a nap and remind myself that I can't do it all. Not even close.

You might be juggling kids or work or other responsibilities, perhaps all three. Here I share with you some of the ways that I fit writing into my life in case any of it is helpful for you.

Tips for Juggling Responsibilities and Writing

1. I set my alarm and get up before my kids. This was impossible when they were little because they got up

so silly-early, but it works now and gives me an hour to write before the days thunder on.

2. My kids read my drafts. I ask my daughter to give me feedback. It gives her editorial power and me an opportunity to connect with her. She loves to spot typos and to tell me what's not working for her. She's my favourite editor (although I love all the editors I've ever worked with. They've all brought amazing insight to my work).

3. I accept that I can't go to every reading or class or even award ceremony, however much I might want to (I had to ask someone else to accept the Arthur Ellis Award for me because I was deep in small children). My friend in the UK, also called Ali, reminded me that this period of my life is only a season (a long season, true—I think there were at least eight years when I was either breastfeeding or holding a baby). Already, my teenager is off in his own life (and bedroom) and barely tolerates my existence. Time will come round again when I can write more. And this thought helps me accept the things I feel I can't get to right now as a writer.

4. I watch enjoyable movies designed for young adults with my kids. My daughter and I watched some of *Wednesday* together. All in the name of work, right?

5. I do a lot more prewriting now. By structuring and reflecting on the shape of my story, I save myself a couple of drafts at least. I hope the tips and ideas in this book will do the same for you.

6. Some days, I let it go. Dealing with life and work and whatever else is on your plate is sometimes enough. Writing is there for you as a creative practice, not as something else on a relentless to-do list.

7. I miss social events. I don't watch much on TV. I sometimes go for weeks without doing any sort of exercise. I forget important dates. I let people down. I drop the ball. Often. I have got good at apologizing.

8. I say no to things. I frame it to myself as: I'm saying yes to all the other stuff I have to do. And then I say no. Often I apologize and sometimes I end up saying yes, even when I don't have time at all. It's not a perfect system, but it helps.

CONFIDENCE AND WRITER'S BLOCK

For years, when people asked me about writer's block, I'd reply glibly, "Barbara Kingsolver says, 'I have three children, I don't have time for writer's block.'" Except, it seems that wherever I got the quotation from doesn't exist. Barbara Kingsolver doesn't have three children, and I seem to have fabricated some sort of meaning from a made-up phrase.

As I've been living a writing life longer, I've learned that there are patches of time where it's impossible to write. Maybe life has thrown stuff at you so intensely that the idea of writing falls flat. My dad had an awful accident riding a horse, which led to him having emergency surgery for a brain bleed. My heart in my mouth, no writing happened until I knew he'd survived. The same for each of his subsequent surgeries. His advice to me has always been to "be gentle with yourself," and so I take this to heart when I need a break.

Conversely, when life is busy, finding time to write becomes a priority for me. Writing itself makes me more able to cope and less likely to drop the ball. There's something meditative and peaceful about writing, for me, and earning those days when the words flow and the story comes alive are worth the early mornings and snatched windows of time. That's what Barbara Kingsolver's not-quotation meant to me—in the moments when I do find time to write, I don't have time to be blocked.

But while I don't have time to be blocked, sometimes my confidence flags. And when my confidence flags, even if I don't think I have time to be blocked, I get stuck. That happens less often now. And that's not because of the books I've published. They made me *more* focused on what other people thought about my writing. Interestingly it was the rejections that helped me become more confident.

Let me explain. It goes back to the purpose of writing, which I thought I knew when I was on that boat in Indonesia so many years ago. As I've done this more and more, the purpose of writing has become clearer for me. Writing opens up the world. It creates and invites conversations with other people, it forges connections, and it helps me understand and interpret the world I live in. My purpose, as I shared at the beginning, was originally publication because I wanted validation. Now I seek to share my books with the world because of the conversations I want to be able to have. Firstly, with an editor, and then, most importantly, with my readers. I want to talk about the things I'm passionate about—how social media tells stories, how AI is changing the world, how we steal identities, the impact of crime on a community, what our shadow selves are like, what anxiety and ADHD are like to live with for a parent. And some of my writing is just for me. I don't want to edit it. I don't want to talk about it. I just want to write it. That writing serves a purpose for me, too, because my overall aim is to feel that internal measure of satisfaction with my own words, line by line, story by story, conversation by conversation.

Confidence comes and goes. Some days are awful and some days are wonderful. In writing and in life. Showing up for the page is how the world makes sense for me.

Tips for When Your Confidence Flags and You're Feeling Blocked

When you're feeling a loss of confidence and are blocked, please come back to these questions: What are you passionate about? What do you want to share with others? What sparks your curiosity and makes you come alive?

Writer's block can be very real and very unpleasant, but usually when the external world is blocked out and you sit with your own need to get into flow, you can ignite that fire again. Writing is likely your primary flow activity. Try writing to get into flow, not for any other goal.

Find an hour that you can repeat every day. Put the world away from your blank page. Free write until you feel ready to do all the other pieces again.

FINAL WORDS

I've shared with you everything I know about writing so far, but by the time it gets into your hands, I hope to have learned more. Writing is always an opportunity to learn more. It would be boring to me if it were easy or repetitive, and every book I write gives me an opportunity to learn anew.

Sharing what I know so you can write your best work is a privilege and it also teaches me more about this beautiful writing life I'm so amazed I get to live.

What I want for you is that the stories in your heart arrive on the page where you want them to be. Maybe one day I'll get to read your words. I hope so.

CHAPTER 13 EXERCISES

Practical Task

Take a look online at some of your favourite authors for young readers. How do they share their books and writing lives? Write a list of your favourite platforms and think about how you could use them more to share your writing self.

Writing: 10 Minutes

I'd love you to keep freewriting and playing as a writer, even as you finish a book and submit work. Ideally, you have work out on submission while you keep writing—a new book, perhaps, but just keep writing as part of your life even if the idea of writing another book isn't where you're at.

For today, write for ten minutes using the prompt: *as soon as it was open (name) realized it was a mistake…*

Writing: 30 Minutes

Write about what you've discovered about your writing self as you've read this book. If you like, share it with me online.

Taking It Further

It's so hard for me to finish a book on writing for you, because I believe there's always so much more to say that's bespoke to each individual author. I share a lot online regularly about writing and how it's going for me, so come and find me there. As I write more, I learn more, and I love helping other writers on the page. The rest of this book is full of great books for you to read and resources for you to explore.

PLACES TO GO:
FURTHER READING

(Alphabetical by author)

PICTURE BOOKS TO GET YOU EXCITED

Ada Twist, Scientist by Andrea Beaty, illustrated by David Roberts (I love the rest of the books in this series, too)

Moo, Baa, La La La! by Sandra Boynton (or anything by Sandra!)

Imani's Moon by JaNay Brown-Wood, illustrated by Hazel Mitchell

Jamberry by Bruce Degen

The Paper Dolls by Julia Donaldson, illustrated by Rebecca Cobb (or anything by Julia!)

Penguin by Polly Dunbar

Birdsong by Julie Flett (or anything written or illustrated by Julie!)

Where Is the Green Sheep by Mem Fox (this one is wonderful for rhyme and rhythm)

Oh No, George! by Chris Haughton (my absolute favourite, but everything else by Chris, too)

Lost and Found by Oliver Jeffers (or anything by Oliver, but particularly look at his illustrations!)

Fox and Bear by Miriam Körner

Ida, Always by Caron Levis, illustrated by Charles Santoso (a superb exploration of how a picture book can handle grief)

The Wish Tree Aby Kyo Maclear (or anything by Kyo, especially her picture book biographies!)

Goodbye Autumn, Hello Winter by Kenard Pak (for stunning illustrations)

This Is It by Daria Peoples-Riley

A Different Pond by Bao Phi

The New Baby Calf by Edith Newlin Chase, illustrated by Barbara Reid (or anything illustrated or written by Barbara!)

Be You by Peter H. Reynolds (he's a wonderful illustrator and author)

The Stone Thrower by Jael Ealey Richardson, illustrated by Matt James (I love *Because You Are*, too!)

On the Trapline or *When We Were Alone* by David A. Robertson (or anything by David!)

Where the Wild Things Are by Maurice Sendak

The Cat in the Hat by Dr. Seuss (and everything else written by Dr. Seuss too!)

The Most Magnificent Thing by Ashley Spires (this is such a huge hit in our house)

Tiny T. Rex by Jonathan Stutzman (I especially like this for its clear three-act structure)

Wishes by Muon Thi Van, illustrated by Victo Ngai

We Sang You Home by Richard Van Camp (or anything by Richard—I love his work *so* much!)

That's Not My Kitten by Fiona Watt, illustrated by Rachel Wells

Knuffle Bunny by Mo Willems (anything by Mo, especially his books for readers who are starting to read for themselves, like *Elephant and Piggy*)

Bear Wants More by Karma Wilson, illustrated by Jane Chapman (or anything by Karma, for rhyme and rhythm)

Goodnight Moon by Margaret Wise Brown, illustrated by Clement Hurd

In My Heart by Jo Witek, illustrated by Christine Roussey (a favourite in our home to talk about feelings)

CHAPTER BOOKS

Younger Chapter Books

For ages 5 to 8 or 6 to 9, though older kids may enjoy them too!

The Fabled Stables series by Jonathan Auxier, illustrated by Olga Demidova

The Miniature World of Marvin and James by Elise Broach, illustrated by Kelly Murphy

Biscuit by Alyssa Satin Capucilli, illustrated by Pat Schories

Our Friend Hedgehog series by Lauren Castillo

The Bolds series by Julian Cleary (Oh, these books make us laugh so much!)

Magic School Bus First Readers by Joanna Cole

The Notebook of Doom series by Troy Cummings

Yasmin series by Saadia Faruqi, illustrated by Hatem Aly

The Kids of the Polk Street School series by Patricia Reilly Giff, illustrated by Blanche Sims

Zigzag Kids series by Patricia Reilly Giff, illustrated by Alasdair Bright

The Princess in Black series by Shannon Hale and Dean Hale, illustrated by LeUyen Pham

King & Kayla series by Dori Hillestad Butler, illustrated by Nancy Meyers

Frog and Toad series by Arnold Lobel

Stink and the Incredible Super-Galactic Jawbreaker by Megan McDonald, illustrated by Peter H. Reynolds

The Kingdom of Wrenly (whole series) by Jordan Quinn, illustrated by Robert McPhillips

Junie B. Jones and the Stupid Smelly Bus by Barbara Park, illustrated by Denise Brunkus

Monkey Me series by Timothy Roland

Like Pickle Juice on a Cookie by Julie Sternberg, illustrated by Matthew Cordell

Nate the Great series by Marjorie Weinman Sharmat, illustrated by Marc Simont

Dragon Masters series by Tracey West, illustrated by Graham Howells and Damien Jones

Older Chapter Books

For ages 7 to 10, these books have plots and humour that appeal to the older end of the chapter book market, though younger kids may enjoy them, too!

Ivy + Bean series by Annie Barrows, illustrated by Sophie Blackall

Little Dog, Lost by Marion Dane Bauer, illustrated by Jennifer A. Bell

Bad Kitty series by Nick Bruel

Mermaid Tales series by Debbie Dadey, illustrated by Tatevik Avakyan

The Adventures of the Bailey School Kids series by Debbie Dadey and Marcia Thornton Jones, illustrated by John Steven Gurney (now made into a graphic novel series by Angeli Rafer!)

Geronimo Stilton series by Elisabetta Dami (these cross from younger chapter books to older)

Amber Brown series by Paula Danziger, illustrated by Tony Ross

The Whipping Boy by Sid Fleischmann, illustrated by Peter Sis (crosses over to lower middle grade)

The Traveling Circus by Marie-Louise Gay and David Homel

Mr. Macky Is Wacky by Dan Gutman, illustrated by Jim Paillot

Mighty Monty by Johanna Hurwitz, illustrated by Anik McGrory

Toys Go Out by Emily Jenkins, illustrated by Paul O. Zelinsky

Polly Diamond series by me, Alice Kuipers, illustrated by Diane Toledano

Mindy Kim series by Lyla Lee, illustrated by Dung Ho

Gooney Bird Greene by Lois Lowry, illustrated by Middy Thomas

Mrs. Piggle-Wiggle by Betty MacDonald, illustrated by Alexandra Boiger

Judy Moody series by Megan McDonald, illustrated by Peter H. Reynolds

Clementine series by Sara Pennypacker, illustrated by Marla Frazee (these have substantial text and could be considered very early middle grade, but stories appeal to the chapter book crowd)

Sideways Stories from Wayside School series by Louis Sachar, illustrated by Adam McCauley (crosses over to early middle grade)
Time Twisters series by Steve Sheinkin, illustrated by Neil Swaab (combines fiction and non-fiction)
Diary of an Ice Princess series by Christina Soontornvat
Skunk and Badger by Amy Timberlake, illustrated by Jon Klassen

Graphic Chapter Books

Chronicles of Claudette series by Jorge Aguirre, illustrated by Rafael Rosado
Narwhal and Jelly series by Ben Clanton
The Princess and the Frog by Will Eisner
Bug Boys series by Laura Knetzger
Hildafolk series by Luke Pearson
Captain Underpants series by Dav Pilkey
Phoebe and Her Unicorn series by Dana Simpson
Bone series by Jeff Smith
Binky the Space Cat series by Ashley Spires
Plants vs. Zombies series by Paul Tobin, illustrated by Ron Chan

MIDDLE GRADE

Younger Middle Grade

These books may appeal to older chapter book readers. Many of them have a few black-and-white illustrations but are longer texts than standard chapter books and so are moving into middle grade territory. But they're worth adding to your reading list because they are wonderful examples of terrific characters, plots, and writing.

Ramona Forever by Beverly Cleary, illustrated by Alan Tiegreen (the Beezus and Ramona books straddle the chapter book/early middle grade categories)

Fantastic Mr. Fox by Roald Dahl, illustrated by Quentin Blake (or any of Roald's books, including *George's Marvelous Medicine*, *Matilda*, and *Charlie and the Chocolate Factory*)

Flora and Ulysses by Kate DiCamillo, illustrated by K.G. Campbell

The Tale of Despereaux by Kate Dicamillo, illustrated by Timothy Basil Ering

Stella Diaz series by Angela Dominguez

Ways to Make Sunshine by Renée Watson, illustrated by Nina Mata

Classic Middle Grade

For readers ages 8 to 12.

Izzy Kline Has Butterflies by Beth Ain (novel in verse)

The House with Chicken Legs by Sophie Anderson

Mr. Popper's Penguins by Florence and Richard Atwater

The Name of This Book Is Secret by Pseudonymous Bosch (and the other books by this mysterious author, who, similar to Lemony Snicket, uses the author-as-character technique in the storytelling)

Al Capone Does My Shirts and *Al Capone Does My Homework* by Gennifer Choldenko

Moo by Sharon Creech

James and the Giant Peach and *Matilda* by Roald Dahl (anything by Roald Dahl is a hit with younger middle grade readers)

Superstar by Mandy Davis

Harriet the Spy by Louise Fitzhugh

Anne Frank: The Diary of a Young Girl by Anne Frank (for readers at the older end)
Joey Pigza Swallowed the Key by Jack Gantos
Elidor by Alan Garner
Real Friends by Shannon Hale and LeUyen Pham
Bunnicula by Deborah and James Howe (lower end of middle grade)
When You Trap a Tiger by Tae Keller
Hello, Universe by Erin Entrada Kelly
Icefall by Matthew J. Kirby
World's Worst Parrot by Alice Kuipers (hi-lo book, meaning it's a high-interest novel for readers age 8–12 who are reading at about a second- or third-grade reading level)
Audacity Jones to the Rescue by Kirby Larsen
Hattie Big Sky by Kirby Larsen
Ella Enchanted by Gail Carson Levine
Capture the Flag by Kate Messner
Willa and the Whale by Chad Morris and Shelly Brown
Wish by Barbara O'Connor
Wonder by R.J. Palacio
Bridge to Terabithia by Katherine Paterson
The First Rule of Punk by Celia C. Pérez
All the Greys on Greene Street by Laura Tucker
The Lost Girl by Anne Ursu
Other Words for Home by Jasmine Warga
Charlotte's Web by E.B. White (though the writing style is not contemporary, if you've never read this book, it's still a wonderful example of plot and characters for younger middle grade readers)
Clayton Byrd Goes Underground by Rita Williams-Garcia
The Book Thief by Marcus Zusak (which adults also love!)

Series for Younger Middle Grade

For ages 8 to 12.

The Mighty Muskrats Mystery series by Michael Hutchinson
Starring Jules series by Beth Ain
Chasing Vermeer series by Blue Balliett, illustrated by Brett Helquist
The Bad Guys series by Aaron Blabey
All Four Stars series by Tara Dairman
Spiderwick Chronicles series by Toni DiTerlizzi and Holly Black
The Home-Front Heroes series by Teresa R. Funke
Greystone Secrets series by Margaret Peterson Haddix
Diary of a Wimpy Kid series by Jeff Kinney
The Chronicles of Narnia series by C.S. Lewis
The Doll People series by Ann M. Martin and Laura Godwin, illustrated by Brett Helquist (younger middle grade)
The Winnie Years series by Lauren Myracle
Middle School series by James Patterson (also check out his I Funny series and his Treasure Hunters series)
The Fourth Stall series by Chris Rylander
A Series of Unfortunate Events series by Lemony Snicket (this is a pen name, which is an interesting storytelling technique), illustrated by Brett Helquist
The Gaither Sisters trilogy by Rita Williams-Garcia

Older Middle Grade

For ages 10 to 14. Middle-grade type characters and conflicts, but with slightly more complex plots that appeal to readers who are not yet ready for YA topics but who have outgrown traditional middle grade stories (for example, middle school stories instead of

> *elementary school settings). Characters may be up to age 14 but are still emotionally and socially dealing with solid middle grade issues. Sometimes the characters are contemplating* YA *conflicts but not actually tackling them yet. These books are often a bit too sophisticated for the younger end of the middle grade audience—readers ages 8 to 9. They may also appeal to* YA *readers who want lighter fare, or who are reluctant readers.*

The Line Tender by Kate Allen
The One and Only Ivan by Katherine Applegate
The Girl Who Drank the Moon by Kell Barnhill
The Next Great Paulie Fink and *The Thing About Jellyfish* by Ali Benjamin
Are You There God? It's Me, Margaret by Judy Blume (a classic that helped define middle grade fiction)
Greetings from Witness Protection! by Jake Burt
Summerlost by Ally Condie
New Kid by Jerry Craft
Cyclone by Doreen Cronin
Blended by Sharon M. Draper
How to Survive Middle School by Donna Gephart
George by Alex Gino
To Night Owl from Dogfish by Holly Goldberg Sloan and Meg Wolitzer
Allies by Alan Gratz
Hoot by Carl Hiaasen
The Seventh Wish by Kate Messner
Hatchet by Gary Paulsen
Pax by Sara Pennypacker, illustrated by Jon Klassen (this book really spans upper middle grade into YA readers)
Ghost by Jason Reynolds

Holes by Louis Sachar
The Warden's Daughter and *Wringer* by Jerry Spinelli
When You Reach Me by Rebecca Stead
Feathers and *Brown Girl Dreaming* by Jacqueline Woodson
Front Desk by Kelly Yang

Series for Older Middle Grade

For ages 10 to 14.

The Goblin trilogy by Hilari Bell
Raymie Nightingale trilogy by Kate DiCamillo
The Quantum League series and the Dark Gravity Sequence series by Matthew J. Kirby
Percy Jackson and the Olympians series by Rick Riordan, or any of Rick's series, including The Trials of Apollo, The Heroes of Olympus, and Magnus Chase. These are plot-driven adventure stories, so they also appeal to young adult readers, as well as skilled readers in the lower end of middle grade.
The Misewa Saga series by David Robinson
The Harry Potter series by J.K. Rowling (this series really appeals to middle grade and younger YA readers alike, as Harry ages as the series progresses)

Graphic Novels for Middle Grade Readers

This Was Our Pact by Ryan Andrews
El Deafo by Cece Bell (spans the older chapter book/younger middle grade range)
The Graveyard Book by Neil Gaiman, adapted and illustrated by P. Craig Russell
One Trick Pony by Nathan Hale

Snow White: A Graphic Novel by Matt Phelan
Sidekicks by Dan Santat
Fish Girl by David Wiesner and Donna Jo Napoli
American Born Chinese by Gene Luen Yang

YOUNG ADULT

Young Adult for Ages 12 and Up

While middle school includes readers ages 12, 13, and 14, some of these books—depending on the school district—may be considered too "adult" for middle school readers, and so would only be found in high school libraries.

The Poet X by Elizabeth Acevedo
What If It's Us? by Becky Albertalli and Adam Silvera
The Absolutely True Diary of a Part-Time Indian by Sherman Alexie
Fever 1793 by Laurie Halse Anderson
Thirteen Reasons Why by Jay Asher
Forever by Judy Blume
Scarlett Epstein Hates It Here by Anna Breslaw
All-American Girl and *Ready or Not* by Meg Cabot
Tiny Pretty Things and *Shiny Broken Pieces* by Sona Charaipotra and Dhonielle Clayton
An Uninterrupted View of the Sky by Melanie Crowder
Once and For All by Sarah Dessen (all of Sarah Dessen's books have a huge following, especially among YA girls)
Fat Kid Rules the World by K.L. Going
The Fault in Our Stars by John Green (technically older YA, but lots of younger YA readers love this). Also check out his *An Abundance of Katherines*.

Honk If You Hate Me and *Big Mouth* by Deborah Halverson
The Eleventh Plague and *The Darkest Path* by Jeff Hirsch
Life on the Refrigerator Door by me, Alice Kuipers! (This is the only one I've written of my YA books that is okay for younger readers, and even then it covers dark topics.)
The Downstairs Girl by Stacy Lee
One of Us is Lying by Karen M. McManus
Slay by Brittney Morris
I'll Give You the Sun by Jandy Nelson (this book would also appeal to older YA readers)
We Are All Made of Molecules by Susin Nielsen (this book also appeals to readers in the 10–14 age group)
Pax by Sara Pennypacker, illustrated by Jon Klassen (this book spans upper middle grade into YA readers)
Long Way Down by Jason Reynolds
Opposite of Always by Justin A. Reynolds
How I Live Now by Meg Rosoff
Eleanor & Park by Rainbow Rowell
Crying Laughing by Lance Rubin
Dust, *Tribes*, and *The Hunchback Assignments* by Arthur Slade
Stargirl by Jerry Spinelli
Ordinary Girls by Blair Thornburgh
Code Name Verity by Elizabeth Wein

Series for Ages 12 and Up

Seeds of America trilogy by Laurie Halse Anderson
Knight and Rogue series and The Shield, Sword, and Crown series by Hilari Bell
The Princess Diaries series by Meg Cabot
Mortal Instruments series by Cassandra Clare

The Hunger Games series by Suzanne Collins
Assassin's Creed series by Matthew J. Kirby
The Lunar Chronicles series by Marissa Meyer
The Internet Girls series by Lauren Myracle
Miss Peregrine's Peculiar Children series by Ransom Riggs
Divergent series by Veronica Roth
Dragon Assassin series by Arthur Slade
Unwind Dystology series by Neal Shusterman
An Ember in the Ashes trilogy by Sabaa Tahir
Uglies series by Scott Westerfeld

Older Young Adult

For readers ages 14 and up. The biggest reason for this new age designation is to alert middle school librarians, teachers, and principals that these books are really high school fare. But, depending on the school, you might find some of these titles on middle school shelves.

Speak by Laurie Halse Anderson
Feed by M.T. Anderson
Firekeeper's Daughter by Angeline Boulley
Black Girl Unlimited by Echo Brown
Ready, Player One by Ernest Cline
The Living and *The Hunted* by Matt de la Peña
Saint Anything by Sarah Dessen
The Marrow Thieves by Cherie Dimaline
Before I Die by Jenny Downham
The Last True Poets of the Sea by Julia Drake
Pet by Akwaeke Emezi
I Have Lost My Way by Gayle Forman
Give Me Some Truth by Eric Gansworth

Symptoms of Being Human by Jeff Garvin
Enter Title Here by Rahul Kanakia
Dig by A.S. King
Openly Straight and *Honestly Ben* by Bill Konigsberg
40 Things I Want to Tell You by me, Alice Kuipers! Any of my other YA, too.
Every Day and *Another Day* by David Levithan (check out all of David Levithan's other books, including those he's written with Rachel Cohn)
We Were Liars by E. Lockhart
10 Things I Can See from Here by Carrie Mac
Dumplin' and *Side Effects May Vary* by Julie Murphy
All the Bright Places by Jennifer Niven
Before I Fall by Lauren Oliver
Across the Universe by Beth Revis
All American Boys by Jason Reynolds and Brendan Kiely (anything and everything by Jason Reynolds!)
Patron Saints of Nothing by Randy Ribay
Bone Gap and *Thirteen Doorways, Wolves Behind Them All* by Laura Ruby
Aristotle and Dante Discover the Secrets of the Universe by Benjamin Alire Sáenz
The Hate U Give by Angie Thomas
Just a Normal Tuesday by Kim Turrisi
Frankly in Love by David Yoon
Everything, Everything and *The Sun is Also a Star* by Nicola Yoon
How to Save a Life by Sara Zarr

Series for Ages 14 and Up

Legacy of Orisha series by Tomi Adeyami
The School for Good and Evil series by Soman Chainani
Chemical Garden trilogy by Lauren DeStefano
If I Stay collection by Gayle Forman
To All the Boys I've Loved Before series by Jenny Han
Crank trilogy by Ellen Hopkins
Twilight series by Stephanie Meyer
Chaos Walking series by Patrick Ness
Delirium trilogy by Lauren Oliver
Raven Cycle series and the Shiver trilogy by Maggie Stiefvater (and if you love these, check out her other series)
Daughter of Smoke and Bone trilogy by Laini Taylor
The 5th Wave series by Rick Yancey

Graphic Novels for Young Adult Readers

Yvain: The Knight of the Lion by M.T. Anderson, illustrated by Andrea Offermann
In Real Life by Cory Doctorow, illustrated by Jen Wang
Nimona by ND Stevenson
Laura Dean Keeps Breaking Up with Me by Mariko Tamaki, illustrated by Rosemary Valero-O'Connell
This One Summer by Mariko Tamaki, illustrated by Jillian Tamaki
Blankets by Craig Thompson
Kiss Number 8 by Colleen AF Venable, illustrated by Ellen T. Crenshaw
Spill Zone by Scott Westerfeld, illustrated by Alex Puvilland

BOOKS ABOUT WRITING AND THE CREATIVE PROCESS THAT I LOVE

The Artists' Way: A Spiritual Path to Higher Creativity by Julie Cameron

Story Genius by Lisa Cron

Bird by Bird: Some Instructions on Writing and Life by Anne Lamott

Write Characters Your Readers Won't Forget: A Toolkit for Emerging Writers by Stant Litore

Everyone Has What It Takes: A Writer's Guide to the End of Self-Doubt by William Kenower

Fearless Writing: How to Create Boldly and Write with Confidence by William Kenower

On Writing: A Memoir of the Craft by Stephen King

How to Tell a Story by The Moth

Writing the Other: A Practical Approach by Nisi Shawl and Cynthia Ward

The Science of Storytelling by Will Storr

PLACES TO GO ONLINE

First of all, check out my website: *www.alicekuipers.com*. I regularly share writing and lines from books here: *alicekuipers.substack.com*.

There are a lot of amazing online creative writing classes, but I love what we do at The Novelry for understanding story and structure: *www.thenovelry.com*. You can work with me as a coach, or any of the rest of the terrific team, including editors from the Big Five publishing houses.

Writing the Other offers a great range of courses and direction: *www.writingtheother.com*. Their on-demand webinar will guide you on working with sensitivity readers: *writingtheother.com/sensitivity-readers-webinar*.

I've also learned a lot about writing about diversity with the resources from Writing with Color: *writingwithcolor.tumblr.com/Navigation*.

I've learned a lot from Mary Kole here: *www.marykole.com*.

And don't miss Arthur Slade's website: *www.arthurslade.com/books*.

Here is a list of online editors with Canada's national editors' association, Editors Canada: *www.editors.ca/ode/search*.

CANSCAIP (Canadian Society of Children's Authors, Illustrators, and Performers) gives a lot of tools and support: *www.canscaip.org*. In Saskatchewan we have a conference every second year with CANSCAIP Prairie Horizons: *skcanscaip.wordpress.com*.

Take a look at the work of a range of visual artists here to think about the type of illustrator you may want to work with through Canadian Artists' Representation/Le Front des artistes canadiens (CARFAC): *www.carfac.ca*.

Be sure to check out *Children's Book Insider* for lots of great writing and publishing information (like Above the Slushpile): *www.cbiclubhouse.com*.

Canadian publishers who accept submissions directly from Canadian authors (make sure to check their online submission criteria):

- Orca Book Publishers:
  www.orcabook.com/AuthorGuidelines

- Owlkids Books: *www.owlkidsbooks.com/submissions*
- Red Deer Press (local editor Beverley Brenna is Editorial Director for their children's arm): *www.reddeerpress.com/red-deer-press-submissions*
- Tundra Press: *tundrabooks.com/submissions*

Get to know the work of hybrid publishers by taking a look at Your Nickel's Worth Publishing in Regina, Saskatchewan: *www.ynwp.ca.*

And finally, don't forget to check out Saskatchewan Writers' Guild if you're in the province! It's a not-for-profit cultural organization that acts as an advocate to improve the status of Saskatchewan writers; encourages the development of writers at all levels; and strives to improve public access and awareness to Saskatchewan writers and their work.

ACKNOWLEDGMENTS

I want to thank my agent, Jackie Kaiser, who has guided me for many years, and through many books. A writing life has ups and downs, and she's been there for them all. Thanks, too, to the rest of the hard-working and inspiring WCA team.

Thank you to everyone at University of Regina Press for this beautiful book, especially Shannon Parr, Rachel Stapleton, Jellyn Ayudan, Kelly Laycock, and Jeanette Lynes. Working with you all has been a pleasure and I'm very grateful.

Many people inspire me along the way, reading my words, buying my books, coming to my book launches, sending me messages and supporting me through fourteen published books so far. My local community in Saskatoon is teeming with terrific writers and I want to thank CANSCAIP Prairie Horizons and the SWG for the amazing communities you create for anyone who feels like crafting with words. Thank you, too, to CBI. Laura and Jon have been wonderful for so many years, and they've taught me so much.

Working at The Novelry fills my days with magic and more writing. I love the writers I get to work with, and our coaching and editorial team. All of you inspire me, all the time. And make me laugh quite a lot, too.

When I head to Substack to write and dream, I find connection and community. Thank you to anyone who has taken the time to comment and share with me there. And to my beloved friends all over the world who are all suddenly reading my weekly essays and touching base: thank you.

My writing days are full of fun and family. Thank you to my family in the UK and Switzerland for the weekly calls, the messages, the photos and the love throughout my writing career. Thanks to my wild and wonderful kids for the ideas and the way you make me work hard to be better and do better. And, Yann, thank you for everything you've given me to help me build a life filled with creativity, ideas, and joy.

Tammy Zdunich

Bestselling award-winning author Alice Kuipers has published fourteen books for young readers. Her work is published in 36 countries and she works as a writing coach for The Novelry. She lives in Saskatoon with her four children.

www.alicekuipers.com

Books in University of Regina Press's

WRITERS ON WRITING SERIES

Gather: Richard Van Camp on the Joy of Storytelling
by Richard Van Camp (2021)

Voice: Adam Pottle on Writing with Deafness
by Adam Pottle (2019)

Sleuth: Gaïl Bowen on Writing Mysteries
by Gail Bowen (2018)

The Writers on Writing series offers readers witty, conversational reflections on a wide range of craft-related topics, as well as practical advice for writers and the writing life at any level. The books are accessible and handy, yet they don't shy away from the challenges of writing. They'll become your friends. Think of sitting down in a coffee shop in conversation with a smart, friendly, veteran author. Part inspiration, part advice, part anecdote—total oxygen after all those stuffy writing textbooks.

Series Editor: Jeanette Lynes

For more information on this series,
please contact *uofrpress@uregina.ca*.